ITALS, WASHINGTON, D. C.

THE SACRIFICIAL YEARS

THE SACRIFICIAL YEARS

*A Chronicle of
Walt Whitman's Experiences
in the Civil War*

edited and with an introduction by
JOHN HARMON McELROY

DAVID R. GODINE, PUBLISHER
Boston

First published in 1999 by
David R. Godine, Publisher, Inc.
Box 450
Jaffrey, New Hampshire 03452

*Owing to limitations of space, acknowledgments of reproduced material
appear on page 163.*

Library of Congress Cataloging in Publication Data

Whitman, Walt, 1819-1892.
The sacrificial years : a chronicle of Walt Whitman's experiences in
the Civil War / Walt Whitman ; edited by John Harmon McElroy.
p.   cm.
Includes bibliographical references (p.   ).
1. Whitman, Walt, 1819-1892—Diaries. 2. United States—History—
Civil War, 1861-1865—Personal narratives. 3. United States—History—
Civil War, 1861-1865—War work. 4. Poets, American—19th century—
Diaries. I. McElroy, John Harmon. II. Title.
PS3231.A364 1997
818'.303—DC21
[B]   97-17833 CIP

ISBN 1-56792-079-9 (alk. paper)

First edition, 1999

This book was printed on acid-free paper

Printed in the United States of America

In memory of
my great-great-grandfather
SAMUEL McELROY,
an immigrant nail-maker from Ireland who became
known throughout western Pennsylvania
for his outspoken opposition to slavery,
and my father,
JOHN HENRY McELROY,
an American combat soldier who put his life at risk
to free Europe from Nazi enslavement.

CONTENTS

List of Illustrations   *ix*

Introduction *by John Harmon McElroy*   *xi*

THE SACRIFICIAL YEARS:

Prelude to Service, 1861 and 1862   1

First Year of Service, 1863   15

Second Year of Service, 1864   77

Third Year of Service, 1865   111

Final Year of Service, 1866   151

Sources and Acknowledgments   159

Index   163

LIST OF ILLUSTRATIONS

In text

Walt Whitman in 1862	*frontispiece*
Walt Whitman ca. 1860	xxi
First Battle of Bull Run	2
The Capitol Dome under construction	16
Christian Commission certificate	45
The "Gettysburg Address" (facsimile)	78
"The Letter for Home"	110
Page from *Drum-Taps*	112
Draft of "O Captain! My Captain!"	130 *and* 131
Letter to a soldier's parents	139 *and* 140
Attorney General's payroll	147
"The dome-crown'd capitol…"	152
Whitman in 1869	157

Between pages 24 and 25

Walt Whitman in 1862	{ 1 }
George Washington Whitman	{ 2 }
Farmhouse used as a hospital	{ 2 }
Shattered street, Fredericksburg	{ 3 }
Union casualties at a field hospital	{ 4 }
Four-wheeled ambulances and attendants	{ 5 }
Abraham Lincoln	{ 6 }
Open-air field hospital at Savage Station	{ 7 }
Aftermath of the battle at Antietam	{ 7 }
Makeshift shelters on Antietam battlefield	{ 8 }

Between pages 56 and 57

Whitman, "taken from life 1863"	{ 1 }
Lincoln, the "Hoosier Michael Angelo"	{ 2 }
Lincoln's photo, annotated by Whitman	{ 3 }
Trinity Church and Capitol under construction	{ 4 }
Edwin M. Stanton	{ 5 }
Charles Sumner	{ 5 }
Ulysses S. Grant	{ 6 }
Robert E. Lee	{ 6 }
Christian Commission headquarters	{ 7 }
110th Penn. Infantry before Chancellorsville	{ 8 }
Wounded of Chancellorsville recovering	{ 8 }

Between pages 88 and 89

Whitman in 1864	{ 1 }
Dead Union soldier, Gettysburg	{ 2 }
Dead Confederate soldier, Petersburg	{ 3 }
Soldiers who gave Whitman their photos	{ 4 *and* 5 }
Brandy Station in 1863	{ 6 }
Winter quarters at Brandy Station	{ 7 }
Amputee with guitar	{ 8 }

Between pages 120 and 121

Ward K, Armory Square Hospital	{ 1 }
Tent hospital	{ 2 }
Stanton Hospital	{ 3 }
Hospital stewards, 9th corps	{ 4 }
Surgeons, Finlay Hospital	{ 4 }
Quartermaster's Hospital	{ 5 }
Campbell Hospital	{ 5 }
Harewood Hospital	{ 6 }
Ward, Harewood Hospital	{ 7 }
Whitman in 1867	{ 8 }

INTRODUCTION

by John Harmon McElroy

BESIDES BEING THE ONLY WAR in the history of the United States fought between Americans, the Civil War is also unique in having by far the highest proportion of combat casualties of any American conflict. During the war, the Union forces enlisted 2,213,000 men and suffered 422,000 deaths and non-fatal wounds in battle, or one combat casualty for every five men who served.* Only partial data exists for Confederate losses on the battlefields. But the available information and the well-documented valor and aggressiveness of Southerners in the Civil War suggest a ratio of Southern combat casualties at least as high as that for the Northern forces, if not higher.

No other American war approaches this level of sacrifice. The three major wars before the Civil War—the American Revolution, the War of 1812, and the Mexican-American War—saw combat casualties averaging somewhere around 1:22; the two that followed it—World War I and World War II—had ratios of combat casualties of 1:18 and 1:17; and in America's most recent major wars, in Korea and Vietnam, the ratio of killed and wounded among total US armed forces in uniform during those wars was 1:42 and 1:44. Evidently, the Civil War involved a willingness on the part of rank-and-

* U.S. Department of Commerce, *Bureau of the Census, Historical Statistics of the United States, Colonial Times to 1970*, 2 vols. (White Plains: Kraus International Publications, 1989), p. 1140, Series Y856, Y880, and Y882, i.e. 140,414 men killed in battle and 281,881 men non-fatally wounded in battle, for a total of 422,295 combat casualties.

file servicemen to commit themselves with exceptional abandon in combat, battle after battle, and an equally remarkable and sustained willingness on the part of their civilian and military commanders to let the carnage continue from one blood-smeared month to another for four years. The question is, What motivated these Americans to fight on the field of battle with such disregard for their lives?

The men who fought the Civil War had various motives, as men have always had in waging war; but the bedrock issue was the future of the United States of America. Would America continue to be what it had been for nearly three-quarters of a century in 1861—a growing republic of freely constituted states with a rapidly increasing population spreading ever-westward across the continent under the unifying authority of the Constitution ratified in 1788—or, would it split apart into two, much-diminished republics, one of which would permit slavery and make states' rights supreme? Both Unionists and Secessionists felt that they were fighting for freedom and democratic government as established by the American Revolution and the Constitution. And large numbers of men on both sides were grimly determined that their understanding of America would prevail, regardless of whether they personally lived to witness the ultimate victory. In the history of Americans, no other armed struggle but this one has ever aroused so pervasive and so powerful a feeling that America was in immediate peril of being destroyed.

A British observer who visited this country for a firsthand view of the war wrote of the sacrifices being made by the Union army:

> The wounded upon an American battle-field, or in an hospital, manifest a spirit singularly uncomplaining, patient, and cheerful. They are sustained by the conviction that the cause for which they are suffering is worthy of it all. It would be easy to fill a volume with evidences that the wounded soldiers give their limbs and their lives without a grudge. Men who have endured untold agonies say that they have no regrets, as the country must be saved. Dying men declare with their last breath that in this cause they lay down their lives willingly—satisfied if, by living or by dying, they can serve their country. The same spirit animates all

classes. Even mothers whose sons have fallen, and whose loss must darken with sorrow all their remaining years, offer willingly this so costly sacrifice.*

The same willingness to sacrifice themselves likewise animated those Americans who fought for the Confederate understanding of freedom and democratic government.

The Sacrificial Years presents the Civil War experiences of a man uniquely qualified to chronicle the sacrifices. This man was Walt Whitman, the great poet of American democracy, who, starting with his first edition of *Leaves of Grass* in 1855, celebrated in his poetry mankind's ineradicable desire for liberty, the equal worth of all human beings, and the special destiny of the United States as the country that allowed millions of ordinary people to exercise their birthright to freedom under laws made by their elected representatives. Walt Whitman's convictions about freedom, equality, and democratic government were crucially tested by the events of 1861-1865, which threatened to shatter the promise of his beloved America.

Whitman's patriotism was not an abstract emotion. The muse that brought forth his poetry did not live in an ivory tower, above the heat and the sweat of summer harvests in the fields of his native Long Island or the clatter and hustle of the crowded Manhattan streets where he reached his maturity. He was a poet of commonplace material realities and of humanity as found on the farm, in machine shops and foundries, aboard fishing schooners and ferry boats, and inside bawdy houses and family homes in every clime and region of America; of all the pleasant and unpleasant variety among human beings. He embraced, as he said, "multitudes" and mankind *"en masse,"* and accepted whatever he found in them, without discriminating among persons as to their occupations, sex, behavior, races, social levels, or birthplaces. He believed in the sanctity of being, and pronounced everything obvious and good as well as everything hidden and sinister to be necessary and useful, because

* Robert Mackenzie, *America and Her Army* (London: T. Nelson and Sons, 1865), p. 58.

whatever existed, either in nature or in society, partook of the mystery and rightness of God's creation. And he believed in the natural goodness of some things, such as loving another person, and the natural badness of other things, such as treating another human being as an inferior. In his most important poem, "Song of Myself," he said that "All goes onward and outward, nothing collapses, /And to die is different from what any one supposed, and luckier."

Whitman's perspective on the Civil War was formed, however, by more than poetic sensibilities. Before he began his career as a poet at age thirty-six, he had been a reporter and an editor on newspapers in Manhattan, Brooklyn, and New Orleans, and his instincts remained those of a reporter. He therefore brought to the war the interests and habits of a seasoned newspaperman, including an ingrained inquisitiveness, respect for facts, and the ability to look unflinchingly at whatever transpired. His newspaperman's traits, in combination with his empathies as a great poet, enabled him to both observe and appreciate the sacrifices Americans made during the Civil War and to record them in evocative, matter-of-fact prose. And he would attain in his wartime work a vantage point from which to witness the full magnitude of these sacrifices.

Born in 1819 in West Hills, New York, a small farming community on the north shore of Long Island, Whitman was living in Brooklyn when the Civil War broke out. At forty-two, he was past the prime age for military service, but at the peak of his maturity as a man and a poet. Like his fellow American writers Herman Melville and James Russell Lowell, who were born the same year he was, Whitman remained a non-combatant. However, he was not destined to experience the war from the sidelines. In its second year, he unexpectedly found himself volunteering for an arduous service that would make demands on his stamina and determination as real (and in some measure as life-threatening) as those incurred by the battlefield soldiers— among them his younger brother George Washington Whitman.

Virtually every American civilian, North and South, was caught up in the events of the Civil War and the emotions provoked by them, from the moment Confederate forces attacked and occupied Fort Sumter. Walt Whitman was no different in that respect from any other civilian. But a more direct and active involvement in the war began for him with his trip to the battlefront of northern Virginia in December 1862, after George Whitman's name appeared in a Brooklyn newspaper as one of the wounded of the 51st New York Volunteers at the battle of Fredericksburg. When Walt Whitman finally reached the field camp of the 51st in Virginia, after an unsuccessful search for his wounded brother in the base hospitals in Washington, D.C., he discovered to his great relief that George had sustained only a relatively minor facial injury. He stayed on in the camp for several days, living in the tent his brother shared with several other officers of his regiment; and what he saw during those days deeply affected him: the rows of fresh-dug graves, corpses awaiting burial, a heap of severed arms and legs outside a house used as a surgical station, and wounded men lying without blankets on the frost-hard December ground around makeshift field hospitals. What especially affected him was the rough indifference with which the wounded were treated on the railroad flatcar and riverboat that carried some of them and him from northern Virginia back to Washington. In his encounters with these fallen survivors of Fredericksburg, Whitman found that he could not look upon their suffering without speaking a word of encouragement, providing a refreshing drink of water, or spreading a blanket over a man shivering from cold because he was too debilitated to do it himself and too weak even to call to anyone. The scale of such unattended misery moved Whitman, he later wrote, to "a profound conviction of necessity" that he had to do something to relieve it. In the years to come, he would witness the same massive suffering again and again after other big battles in Virginia, Maryland, and Pennsylvania; but he never became inured to it.

Arriving in Washington from Fredericksburg, Whitman obtained a part-time clerkship in the office of the Army Paymaster—the first of three such positions he would have, the other two being at the Indian Bureau and the Attorney General's office. The arrangement allowed him to earn enough to sustain himself from a few hours of work each day, while leaving him plenty of time to visit the wards of the proliferating military hospitals in the District of Columbia. (There would eventually be fifty of them.) Intended mainly to receive the wounded from the numerous battles being fought in the vicinity of Washington, these improvised wartime hospitals set up in tents, hastily built one-story wooden galleries, and public buildings such as the Patent Office also contained some of the worst cases of illness among the soldiers of the Army of the Potomac. Virulent contagious diseases such as typhoid and dysentery were not unknown among the patients of these army hospitals; and during his years as a volunteer nurse, Whitman became seriously ill from exposure to dangerous contagions. (Several of the attendants he came to know during these years actually died from their work in the wards.) When his health failed, Whitman retreated to his family in Brooklyn to recoup his strength, and then returned to Washington. He continued tending the sick and the wounded until the last hospital closed and the last patient was discharged. In the opinion of some who knew him later on, after his health was permanently broken, the rigors of his hospital work in Washington in the years 1863, 1864, 1865, and 1866 induced the paralyzing stroke that in 1873, at age fifty-four, left him an invalid for the remaining nineteen years of his life.

Whitman was physically hearty when he began his service in the hospitals, and his above-average six-foot height made him an imposing man for his day. By temperament he was gregarious and generous, and he had an instinctive knack for comprehending how another person's distress might be relieved. These traits made him a good practical nurse, and the doctors and nurses in charge of the wards he visited soon came to trust him and welcome his help. Once he made up his mind to do this work, he never wavered from his decision. The Civil War military hospitals were not easy places to visit. Yet Whitman did so, week in and week out for over three years, and nursed thousands of patients, some of them grotesquely mutilated, profoundly ill, and dying. He suited his attendance to the particular needs of each. Sometimes he kept all-night vigil at the side of a moribund patient he thought might benefit from his presence.

With some of those he attended, he developed something like the comradeship that arises between veterans who have confronted death together, for death was as inevitable in the hospitals as it was on the battlefield. And, as also happens among veterans, he and the soldiers during the quiet times told each other their experiences. Whitman sometimes recorded what he was told in letters he wrote during the war and in the occasional "memoranda" he made about his work in the hospitals. His instincts as a newspaperman, plus his interest in the American character, made him an eager interviewer of the soldiers he met and an attentive listener to their accounts of their ordeals in the war; his unusual powers of imagination as a poet made what had happened to them a part of his own experience. (He gained further knowledge of the war from a second visit to Union forces encamped in northern Virginia.)

In his volunteer service in the army hospitals, Whitman injured his health and sacrificed years of his prime maturity as a poet. But in remembering those years, he said: "What was a man to do?— there were thousands, tens of thousands, hundreds of thousands needing me—needing all who might come." Not enough persons responded to that need. The hospitals were always shorthanded; and the wounded and sick could not always be properly nursed. Whitman, after he saw how many were being stricken down by the war, faithfully devoted himself to as many of the fallen as he could. He did so because they were suffering human beings, and because they had sacrificed themselves for their country, as they understood their country to be, whether Northerner or Southerner. (Wounded Confederates were sometimes brought into the hospitals in Washington from the battlefields, and Whitman, as his wartime memoranda and letters show, never withheld his sympathy from them because they were "Secesh.") Thousands of individual encounters in the military hospitals with Confederates and Unionists, black soldiers and white, confirmed his faith in democracy as a form of government that depends for its success on the sense of personal responsibility in ordinary people. This was the great lesson of the Civil War for Walt Whitman: It proved the virtue of ordinary human beings, and therefore the soundness of the foundation on which the United States rests.

The war also confirmed his belief, often expressed in his prewar poetry, that physical health is correlated to spiritual well-being. And so, without stint, he expended his vitality on those who had been torn and pierced in the storms of shrapnel and lead, or prostrated by sickness in between the holocausts of battle, so that they might regain their health. He proudly believed his efforts during these years of sacrifice made the difference between life and death for more than one afflicted man—as undoubtedly they did.

Whitman's brother George volunteered during the initial months of the Civil War as a private, saw action in twenty-one engagements, and ended the war as a Lieutenant Colonel—one of the few original enlistees in his regiment to survive in service to the war's end. Walt Whitman during his four years of voluntary service never rose above his self-conferred rank of "Army Hospital Visitor." It was a humble rank, yet one that does honor to his memory.

The following chronicle consists of nearly three hundred selections from Whitman's various prose writings about the Civil War—mostly wartime letters and "memoranda," but also some newspaper pieces and postwar memoirs—that recorded what he saw, heard, felt, and thought month by month during his service in the war.* The passages selected have been arranged in the chronological sequence of the events they refer to (rather than, in some cases, when they were written) in order to construct a semblance of the diary Whitman regretted not having kept during that period. His two Civil War notebooks—only partially published when they were removed from the Library of Congress half a century ago, and not recovered until 1995—have also been studied; and some unpublished passages from them used. The source of each selection is given in an Appendix.

A century ago, in 1898, Richard Bucke published fifty-nine letters Whitman wrote during eighteen of the forty-eight months of the war (all but five of them to his mother) and three of his newspa-

---

* Ten years after the Civil War, Whitman published at his own expense in an edition of thirty-two copies fifty-five pages of his notes, titled *Memoranda During the War*. A facsimile of this work, edited by Roy P. Basler, was issued by Indiana University Press in 1962 in observation of the Civil War Centennial.

per articles on the war, under the title *The Wound-Dresser.* Six decades ago, in 1933, Charles Glicksberg published a miscellaneous, topically organized assemblage of Whitman's Civil War prose and poems, *Walt Whitman and the Civil War,* to make more widely available to students and scholars some materials previously unpublished. And thirty-seven years ago, in 1960, the poet Walter Lowenfels republished much of those previous collections, with a little additional prose and poetry (arranged in fourteen categories), as *Walt Whitman's Civil War.* The present work draws on the first two of those works and more recent scholarly editions—most notably the collected writings of Whitman that New York University Press began publishing in the early 1960s—but for the entirely different purpose of presenting the first selective and chronologically comprehensive account of Whitman's experiences in the Civil War, from April 1861 when the fighting started until the last of the military hospitals closed in 1866. Whitman's wartime letters to his mother as collected by Bucke, though making a coherent volume, presented a limited and incomplete account of his experiences in the Civil War, being mostly one set of letters to one person over a period of a year and a half; the Glicksberg and Lowenfels compilations, because they mixed poetry and prose and separated their materials by topic, thwart the reader interested in having a diary-like narrative. I hope that *The Sacrificial Years* provides such a narrative.

Gay Wilson Allen, Roger Asselineau, Helen Britten, Kevin Button, Sam Daniel, David R. Godine, Marilyn Iback, Maja Keech, Ruth Kinnettel, Jerome Loving, Onyria McElroy, William and Irene McElroy, Tenney Nathanson, Margaret O'Neil, Mark Polizzotti, Maj. William D. Tackenberg, Rudy Troike, Christina Ward, and Douglas Winterich provided much-needed advice, encouragement, logistical and computer support, secretarial and editorial help, and curatorial services during the creation and production of *The Sacrificial Years.* Each of them deserves and has my thanks.

J.H.M.
Tucson, 1997

Walt Whitman ca. 1860,
the year before the Civil War began.

THE SACRIFICIAL YEARS

Prelude to Service, 1861 and 1862

The first Battle of Bull Run, July 1861, from a period engraving.

NEWS OF THE ATTACK on fort Sumter and *the flag* at Charlestown harbor, S.C., was receiv'd in New York City late at night (13th April, 1861,) and was immediately sent out in extras of the newspapers. I had been to the opera in Fourteenth street that night, and after the performance was walking down Broadway toward twelve o'clock, on my way to Brooklyn, when I heard in the distance the loud cries of the newsboys, who came presently tearing and yelling up the street, rushing from side to side even more furiously than usual. I bought an extra and cross'd to the Metropolitan hotel (Niblo's) where the great lamps were still brightly blazing, and, with a crowd of others, who gather'd impromptu, read the news, which was evidently authentic. For the benefit of some who had no papers, one of us read the telegram aloud, while all listen'd silently and attentively. No remark was made by any of the crowd, which had increas'd to thirty or forty, but all stood a minute or two, I remember, before they dispers'd.

Even after the bombardment of Sumter, however, the gravity of the revolt, and the power and will of the slave States for a strong and continued military resistance to national authority, were not at all realized at the North, except by a few. Nine-tenths of the people of the free States look'd upon the rebellion, as started in South Carolina, from a feeling one-half of contempt, and the other half composed of anger and incredulity. It was not thought it would be join'd in by Virginia, North Carolina, or Georgia. A great and cautious national official predicted that it would blow over "in sixty days," and folks generally believ'd the prediction. I remember talking about it on a Fulton ferry-boat with the Brooklyn mayor, who said he only "hoped the Southern fire-eaters would commit some overt act of resistance, as they would then be at once so effectually squelch'd, we would never hear of secession again—but he was afraid they never would have the pluck to really do anything." I remember, too, that a couple of companies of the Thirteenth Brooklyn, who rendezvou'd at the city armory, and started thence as thirty days' men, were all provided with pieces of rope, conspicuously tied to their musket-barrels, with which to bring back each man a prisoner from the audacious South, to be led in a noose, on our men's early and triumphant return!

3

Battle of Bull Run, July, 1861

All this sort of feeling was destin'd to be arrested and revers'd by a terrible shock—the battle of first Bull Run—certainly, as we now know it, one of the most singular fights on record. (All battles, and their results, are far more matters of accident than is generally thought; but this was throughout a casualty, a chance. Each side supposed it had won, till the last moment. One had, in point of fact, just the same right to be routed as the other. By a fiction, or series of fictions, the national forces at the last moment exploded in a panic and fled from the field.) The defeated troops commenced pouring into Washington over the Long Bridge at daylight on Monday, 22nd—day drizzling all through with rain.... The men appear, at first sparsely and shame-faced enough, then thicker, in the streets of Washington—appear in Pennsylvania avenue, and on the steps and basement entrances. They come along in disorderly mobs, some in squads, stragglers, companies. Occasionally, a rare regiment, in perfect order, with its officers (some gaps, dead, the true braves,) marching in perfect silence, with lowering faces, stern, weary to sinking, all black and dirty, but every man with his musket, and stepping alive;

but these are the exceptions. Sidewalks of Pennsylvania avenue, Fourteenth street, &c., crowded, jamm'd with citizens, darkies, clerks, everybody, lookers-on; women in the windows, curious expressions from faces, as those swarms of dirt-cover'd return'd soldiers there (will they never end?) move by; but nothing said, no comments; half our lookers-on secesh of the most venomous kind—they say nothing; but the devil snickers in their faces. During the forenoon Washington gets all over motley with these defeated soldiers—queer-looking objects, strange eyes and faces, drench'd (the steady rain drizzles on all day) and fearfully worn, hungry, haggard, blister'd in the feet. Good people (but not over-many of them either,) hurry up something for their grub. They put wash-kettles on the fire, for soup, for coffee. They set tables on the sidewalks—wagon-loads of bread are purchas'd, swiftly cut in stout chunks. Here are two aged ladies, beautiful, the first in the city for culture and charm, they stand with store of eating and drink at an improvis'd table of rough plank, and give food, and have the store replenish'd from their house every half-hour all that day; and there in the rain they stand, active, silent, white-hair'd, and give food, though the tears stream down their cheeks, almost without intermission, the whole time. Amid the deep excitement, crowds and motion, and desperate eagerness, it seems strange to see many, very many, of the soldiers sleeping—in the midst of all, sleeping sound. They drop down anywhere, on the steps of houses, up close by the basements or fences, on the sidewalk, aside on some vacant lot, and deeply sleep.... Meantime, in Washington, among the great persons and their entourage, a mixture of awful consternation, uncertainty, rage, shame, helplessness, and stupefying disappointment. The worst is not only imminent, but already here. In a few hours—perhaps before the next meal—the secesh generals, with their victorious hordes, will be upon us. The dream of humanity, the vaunted Union we thought so strong, so impregnable—lo! it seems already smash'd like a china plate. One bitter, bitter hour— perhaps proud America will never again know such an hour. She must pack and fly—no time to spare. Those white palaces—the dome-crown'd capitol there on the hill, so stately over the trees— shall they be left—or destroy'd first? For it is certain that the talk among certain of the magnates and officers and clerks and officials everywhere, for twenty-four hours in and around Washington after Bull Run, was loud and undisguised for yielding out and out, and substituting the southern rule, and Lincoln promptly abdicating and departing. If the secesh officers and forces had immediately follow'd, and by a bold Napoleonic movement had enter'd Washington the first day, (or even the second,) they could have had things their own way, and a powerful faction north to back them....

4

But the hour, the day, the night pass'd, and whatever returns, an hour, a day, a night like that can never again return. The President, recovering himself, begins that very night—sternly, rapidly sets about the task of reorganizing his forces, and placing himself in positions for future and surer work. If there were nothing else of Abraham Lincoln for history to stamp him with, it is enough to send him with his wreath to the memory of all future time, that he endured that hour, that day, bitterer than gall—indeed a crucifixion day—that it did not conquer him—that he unflinchingly stemm'd it, and resolv'd to lift himself and the Union out of it.

Then the great New York papers at once appear'd, (commencing that evening, and following it up the next morning, and incessantly through many days afterwards,) with leaders that rang out over the land with the loudest, most reverberating ring of clearest bugles, full of encouragement, hope, inspiration, unfaltering defiance. Those magnificent editorials! they never flagg'd for a fortnight. The "Herald" commenced them—I remember the articles well. The "Tribune" was equally cogent and inspiriting—and the "Times," "Evening Post," and other principal papers, were not a whit behind. They came in good time, for they were needed. For in the humiliation of Bull Run, the popular feeling north, from its extreme of superciliousness, recoil'd to the depth of gloom and apprehension.

U.S. Volunteers in the Broadway Hospital
(Opposite the head of Pearl Street)

There is something especially melancholy in the sight presented in the groups of sick United States soldiers, mostly in the North Building—which is exclusively devoted to them. A very large proportion of them are robust-framed young men from the country—from northern New York, and from Maine, New Hampshire, Vermont, and so on.

I have spent two or three Sunday afternoons of late in going around among these sick soldiers, just to help cheer and change a little the monotony of their sickness and confinement—and indeed, just as much, too, for the melancholy entertainment and friendly interest and sympathy, I found aroused in myself toward and among the men. Many of them have no relatives or acquaintances at all in New York, and time moves on slowly and dully enough to them....

One Sunday night, in a ward in the South Building, I spent one of the most agreeable evenings of my life amid such a group of seven convalescent young soldiers of a Maine regiment. We drew around together, on our chairs, in the dimly-lighted room, and after interchanging the few magnetic remarks that show people it is well for them to be together, they told me their stories of country life and adventures, &c., away up there in the Northeast. They were to leave the next day in a vessel for the Gulf, where their regiment was; and they felt so happy at the prospect. I shook hands with them all round at parting, and I know we all felt as if it were the separation of old friends.

There is a lady comes from time to time, quiet and without any fuss, here among the sick and lonesome volunteers. She brings illustrated and other papers, books of stories, little comforts in the way of eating and drinking, shirts, gowns, handkerchiefs, &c.... I see evidences of her having been there, almost always, on my visits. Doctor Hogan has several times mentioned her to me, and so has the excellent Mrs. Mack, the nurse; and often and often have the soldiers mentioned her, and shown me something she has given them....

There are other good, benevolent women who come or send here—and men, too.

6

Left Brooklyn for Falmouth, Va. Dec. 16, 1862—Washington Dec. 17 —[arrived] Falmouth camp of 51st N.Y.V. Dec. 19th '62—

7

...found George alive and well.... [On the way here] I put in about three days of the greatest suffering I ever experienced in my life.... I had my pocket picked in a jam and hurry, changing cars, at Philadelphia—so that I landed [in Washington] without a dime. The next two days I spent hunting through the hospitals, walking day and night, unable to ride, trying to get information—trying to get access to big people, etc.—I could not get the least clue to anything. Odell would not see me at all. But Thursday afternoon, I lit on a way to get down on the Government boat that runs to Aquia creek, and so by railroad to the neighborhood of Falmouth, opposite Fredericksburg—so by degrees I worked my way to Ferrero's brigade, which I found Friday afternoon without much trouble after I got in camp. When I found dear brother George, and found that he was alive and well, O you may imagine how trifling all my cares and difficulties seemed—they vanished into nothing. And now that I have lived for eight or nine days amid such scenes as the camps furnish, and had a practical part in it all, and realize the way that hundreds of thousands of good men are now living, and have had to live for a year or more, not only without any of the comforts, but with death and sickness and hard marching and hard fighting (and no success at that) for their continual experience—really nothing we call trouble seems worth talking about.... While I was there George still lived in Capt. Francis's tent—there were five of us altogether, to eat, sleep, write, etc., in a space twelve feet square, but we got along very well—the weather all along was very fine—and would have got along to perfection, but Capt. Francis is not a man I could like much—I had very little to say to him. George is about building a place, half a hut and half tent, for himself, (he is probably about it this very day,) and then he will be better off, I think. Every captain has a tent, in which he lives, transacts company business, etc., has a cook, (or a man of all work,) and in the same tent mess and sleep his lieutenants, and perhaps the first sergeant. They have a kind of fire-place—and the cook's fire is outside on the open ground.

8

Friday, Saturday, & Sunday, Dec. 19, 20, and 21, was at Falmouth, opposite Fredericksburgh.

The grub was good—had a tip-top time every way.—

...went around among the camps—saw the hard accommodations and experiences of campaign life—the shelter tents—the improvised fireplaces in holes in the ground, with small subterranean passages and small mud chimneys, lengthened out by a barrel with both ends knocked out—Went round mornings and evenings among the men—heard their conversation &c.—the bivouac fires at night, the singing and story telling among the crowded crouching groups.

9

The fenced enclosure in the midst of the woods, for butchering the beef, the just quartered cattle, in huge pieces lying around, the men with rolled up sleeves and stained arms.

10

"Shebangs" the little huts of green boughs, pine or what not, put up for the impromptu shelter of soldiers in Virginia &c.

11

51st N.Y. Col. Ferrero. Started from New York, Oct. 30, '61.—went to Annapolis and laid in the Camp of Instruction two months & six days. Started Jan. 6th '62 in transports for Hatteras—terrible storm & blow, some vessels sunk—short of water & rations—started from

Hatteras Feb. 4th up Pamlico Sound—arrived at Roanoke Feb. 6th, battle of Roanoke,—bombardment of the rebel works, water batteries, by our gun boats. Near all day on the 7th latter part of the day troops landed and Capt. S. Sims & company G. were first ashore, bad weather, rainy miserable weather, no fires would burn &c. men lay in the wet &c.—morning [of the] 8th the battle commenced.— the 51st marched through a horrible swamp to avoid a road battery— the Brooklyn colors were the first planted ashore. The 51st were ordered on in some of the most difficult positions, rebel force 4500 men and several batteries, some of the guns very fine. On the charge, the Brooklyn boys were ahead with the foremost—

Stopt in Roanoke in the barracks till 6th of March—went aboard transports, sailed on the 11th, destination unknown—arrived a Clocum's creek, Neuse river, on the 13th. Landed, formed on the shore (raining like blazes) and started for Newbern 16 miles distant. Passed lately-deserted barracks, earthworks, &c., marched 13 miles and bivouack'd (rain continues, bad as ever)—morn'g of the 14th movement toward Newbern, attack'd the rebels, protected in their breastworks—after 4 hours fighting, the battle was won—(all this was 3 miles from Newbern)—in the affair the 51st lost 103 killed and wounded, 8 of them officers— ...

After Colonel Ferrero was promoted, Lt. Col. Potter became colonel of the regiment, acting for the first time as such at the second battle of Bull Run. On inquiry, I found his chief merits are courage and coolness. When he orders the men to lie down, for protection in an engagement, he will be very likely to walk coolly up and down in front of them, observing operations all around. "Lie down yourself, Colonel," the men will cry out, "some of the rebs will see you." "Yes," he will answer, "but I want to see them too."—The regiment now numbers about 300 men.—on the rolls, 550—started from N.Y. with 1000 total—and have had 80 recruits since....

—[They told me about] eating the green corn—grated through tin pans with rough holes pierced in them—the troops had to do this repeatedly in Virginia, on Pope's retreat—"army pies" and "wash," hard crackers and coffee—"western milk" i.e. whisky (when put in your coffee).

After a march at dusk, in fifteen minutes after the men get the order to halt, they will have their camp fires burning in all directions and the grub in process of cooking, coffee, pork, beef, potatoes boiling, chickens or any thing they stole or grabbed[in any way.

12

My walk out around the camp, the fires burning—groups around— the merry song—the sitting forms—the playing light on the faces— they would tell stories—one would tell a story of a dead man sitting on the top of a rail fence—he had been shot there at sundown, mortally wounded, clung with desperate nerves, and was found sitting there, dead, staring with fixed eyes in the morning—Then I heard of Charley Parker, a young man in Company E. in the 51st; how he was shot on the advance at Fredericksburgh, died hard, suffered much, frothed at the mouth—his body on the return, found entirely stript by the Secesh, and was decently buried by his companions. How he was a noble, beloved young man; one of the soldiers knew his father, and how than Charley no one could possibly be a greater credit to his family. A clean, gallant soul, lad of the 51st; old Brooklyn.

13

The picturesque scene of a battery drill on the open plains, the men at their position, the orders, and signal by trumpet—off they go on a run—
The cannons of pale yellow
—the hurrying horses, the ammunition wagons, carrying an extra wheel behind—some of their horses in the rear.

14

The walk along the Rappahannock in front, a pleasant shore, with trees—See that old town over there—how splintered, bursted, crumbled, the houses—some with their chimneys thrown down—the hospitals—the man with his mouth blown out[.]

Sunday Dec. 21st. Fine pleasant day, bright & sunshining but cool enough to freeze; about 11 o'clock Col. Potter had a regimental inspection, and read the articles of war. The men looked well to me, not in the sense of a march down Broadway, but with the look of men who had long known what real war was, and taken many a hand in [it]—held their own in seven engagements, about a score of skir- mishes &c.—a regiment that had been sifted by death, disablement &c. from eleven hundred men, (including recruits,) down to about two hundred—any one of whom had now an experience, after eigh- teen months, worth more, and more wonderful, than all the romances ever written—…

Begin my visits among the camp hospitals in the army of the Potomac. Spend a good part of the day in a large brick mansion on the banks of the Rappahannock, used as a hospital since the battle—

…the results of the late battle are exhibited everywhere about here in thousands of cases, (hundreds die every day,) in the camp, brigade, and division hospitals. These are merely tents, and some- times very poor ones, the wounded lying on the ground, lucky if their blankets are spread on layers of pine or hemlock twigs, or small leaves. No cots; seldom even a mattress. It is pretty cold. The ground is frozen hard, and there is occasional snow. I go around from one case to another. I do not see that I do much good to these wounded and dying; but I cannot leave them. Once in a while some youngster holds on to me convulsively, and I do what I can for him; at any rate, stop with him and sit near him for hours, if he wishes it.

16

Monday forenoon, Dec. 22.—I write this in the tent of Capt. Sims, of the 51st New York. Sight at the Lacy house—at the foot of tree, immediately in front, a heap of feet, legs, arms, and human frag- ments, cut, bloody, black and blue, swelled and sickening—in the garden near, a row of graves; some distance back, a little while after- wards, I saw a long row of them.…

—Saw the balloon up—a great huge, slow moving thing, with a

curious look to me, as it crawled up, and slanted down again, as if it were alive. The haze, I suppose, prevented any good use—for it staid up only a little while. A beautiful object to me—a graceful, pear-shaped thing, some 30 by 50 feet, (at a guess.) I examined it, by and by, when it was grappled on the ground, in a picturesque ravine, west of Gen. Sumner's headquarters, swelling up there in its diamond-shaped netting, with a watchful sentry over it night and day.

17

Christmas Afternoon, 1862. I write this paragraph in the midst of a large deserted camp ground, with the remains of hundreds of mud-huts, and the debris of an old brigade or division of soldiers all around me. On a road near at hand successive caravans of army wag-ons, some of them apparently interminable, with their six-mule teams, are passing and passing, with only slight intervals, nearly all the time. Not far off is camp of several hundred teamsters with rows and half-moons of wagons ranged around, and heaps of forage, hay, temporary stables, &c. In sight as I sweep my eye over the open ground, (for I can see without obstruction from two to four miles every way) I behold several other such teamsters' camps. Off outside I see the carcases of dead horses and mules. The wooded parts of the surface have been cleared for fuel, & building purposes, for a hun-dred thousand soldiers.... I hear the sound of bugle calls, very mar-tial, at this distance—a fine large troop of cavalry is just passing, the hoofs of the horses shake the ground, and I hear the clatter of sabres. Amid all this pleasant scene, under the sweet sky and warm sun, I sit and think over the battle of last Saturday week.

18

Sight at daybreak—in a camp in front of the hospital tent on a stretcher, (three dead men lying,) each with a blanket spread over him—I lift up one and look at the young man's face, calm and yel-low,—'tis strange!

(Young man: I think this face of yours the face of my dead Christ!)

Early this morning I walked out, in the open fields, one side of the camp. I found some of the soldiers digging graves—they were for the 51st. N.Y. and 11th N.H. There was a row of graves there already, each with a slat of board, generally a piece of barrelhead, on which was inscribed the name of the soldier. Death is nothing here.... All useless ceremony is omitted. (The stern realities of the marches and many battles of a long campaign make the old etiquets a cumber and a nuisance.)

First Year of Service, 1863

View of Washington, D.C., ca. 1862, showing the Capitol dome under construction.

JANUARY

20

Washington. January, '63

—LEFT CAMP AT FALMOUTH, with some wounded, a few days since, and came here by Aquia creek railroad, and so on government steamer up the Potomac. Many wounded were with us on the cars and boat. The cars were just common platform ones. The railroad journey of ten or twelve miles was made mostly before sunrise. The soldiers guarding the road came out from their tents or shebangs of bushes with rumpled hair and half-awake look. Those on duty were walking their posts, some on banks over us, others down far below the level of the track. I saw large cavalry camps off the road. At Aquia creek landing were numbers of wounded going north. While I waited some three hours, I went around among them. Several wanted word sent home to parents, brothers, wives, &c., which I did for them (by mail the next day from Washington.) On the boat I had my hands full. One poor fellow died going up.

I am now remaining in and around Washington, daily visiting the hospitals. Am much in Patent-office, Eighth street, H street, Armory-square, and others. Am now able to do a little good, having money, (as almoner of others home,) and getting experience....

21

One has much to learn in order to do good in these places. Great tact is required. These are not like other hospitals.

…your heart would ache to go through the rows of wounded young men, as I did— …there were about 100 in one long room, just a long shed neatly whitewashed inside. One young man was very much prostrated, and groaning with pain. I stopt and tried to comfort him. He was very sick. I found he had not had any medical attention since he was brought there; among so many he had been overlooked; so I sent for the doctor, and he made an examination of him. The doctor behaved very well—seemed to be anxious to do right—said that the young man would recover; he had been brought pretty low with diarrhoea, and now had bronchitis, but not so serious as to be dangerous. I talked to him some time—he seemed to have entirely given up, and lost heart—he had not a cent of money—not a friend or acquaintance. I wrote a letter from him to his sister—his name is John A. Holmes, Campello, Plymouth county, Mass. I gave him a little change I had—he said he would like to buy a drink of milk when the woman came through with milk. Trifling as this was, he was overcome and began to cry.

23

W.H.E., Co. F., 2d N.J.—His disease is pneumonia. He lay sick at the wretched hospital below Aquia creek, for seven or eight days before brought here. He was detail'd from his regiment to go there and help as nurse, but was soon taken down himself. Is an elderly, sallow-faced, rather gaunt, gray-hair'd man, a widower, with children. He express'd a great desire for good, strong green tea.

24

Bed 3, ward E, Armory, has a great hankering for pickles, something pungent. After consulting the doctor, I gave him a small bottle of horseradish.…

25

In one bed a young man, Marcus Small, company K, 7th Maine—

sick with dysentery and typhoid fever—pretty critical case—I talk with him often—he thinks he will die—looks like it indeed. I write a letter for him home to East Livermore, Maine—I let him talk to me a little, but not much, advise him to keep very quiet—do most of the talking myself—stay quite a while with him, as he holds on to my hand—talk to him in a cheering, but slow, low and measured manner—talk about his furlough, and going home as soon as he is able to travel.

26

Thomas Lindly, 1st Pennsylvania cavalry, shot very badly through the foot—poor young man, he suffers horribly, has to be constantly dosed with morphine, his face ashy and glazed, bright young eyes— I give him a large handsome apple, lay it in sight....

27

Here in this same ward are two young men from Brooklyn, members of the 51st New York. I had known both the two as young lads at home, so they seem near to me. One of them, J.L., lies there with an amputated arm, the stump healing pretty well. (I saw him lying on the ground at Fredericksburgh last December, all bloody, just after the arm was taken off. He was very phlegmatic about it, munching away at a cracker in the remaining hand—made no fuss.) He will recover, and thinks and talks yet of meeting the Johnny Rebs.

28

...as I go for a couple of hours daily, and get to be welcome and useful, I find the masses fully justified by closest contact, never vulgar, ever calm, without greediness, no flummery, no frivolity—responding electric and without fail to affection, yet no whining—not the first unmanly whimper have I yet seen or heard.

29

Frederick Huse, private Co. I. 35th Mass. died in Campbell Hosp.

5th Jan. '63 overdosed by opium pills & laudanum from an ignorant wardmaster.

Joshua Ford, private Co. E. 1st Delaware, wardmaster gave him inwardly muriate of ammonia, intended for a wash for his feet. Jan. 4th '63.

Jan. 13 speak to Penn. ag't. Major Gilliland… about Richard Gardiner, Co. J. 100th Pa. sick in hospital, (bed 39, ward G., Campbell Hospital), his hearing is quite gone—and he has heart disease—is a perfectly fine case for discharge, and wants to be discharged.

30

The grand soldiers are not comprised in those of one side, any more than the other. Here is a sample of an unknown southerner, a lad of seventeen. At the War department, a few days ago, I witness'd a presentation of captured flags to the Secretary. Among others a soldier named Gant, of the 104th Ohio volunteers, presented a rebel battle-flag, which one of the officers stated to me was borne to the mouth of our cannon and planted there by a boy but seventeen years of age, who actually endeavor'd to stop the muzzle of the gun with fence-rails. He was kill'd in the effort….

31

What ought to be done by our family, I feel that *I* am doing, and have done myself. I have made $27 while I have been here, and got the money, and I should think I have paid in little items and purchases and money gifts at least $10 of that to the soldiers—I wouldn't take a thousand dollars for the satisfaction it has been to me—

32

To add to other troubles, amid the confusion of this great army of sick, it is almost impossible for a stranger to find any friend or relative, unless he has the patient's specific address to start upon…. I have known cases, for instance such as a farmer coming here from northern New York to find a wounded brother, faithfully hunting round for a week, and then compell'd to leave and go home without getting any trace of him. When he got home he found a letter from the brother giving the right address.

33

Amory [Hospital] Ward G. bed 7 Jarvis Spaulding, Co. F. 142nd N.Y. from Oswego Co. wants an orange—severe typhoid fever— very low—quite lethargic, needs to be roused.

A young lady who comes here, she brings the illustrated papers— handsome young woman, gliding in and out like an angel.

Armory Hospital, Ward G. bed 8, Henry L. Mitchelle, 5th Conn. Vol. wounded in leg, age 19, has been 5 months in prison in Rich-mond—his description of prison life in R.—was claimed as a deserter from an Alabama regiment and came near being shot—

FEBRUARY

34

Many things invite comment, and some of them sharp criticism, in these hospitals. The Government, as I said, is anxious and liberal in its practice toward its sick; but the work has to be left, in its personal application to the men, to hundreds of officials of one grade or another about the hospitals, who are sometimes entirely lacking in the right qualities. There are tyrants and shysters in all positions, and especially those dressed in subordinate authority. Some of the ward doctors are careless, rude, capricious, needlessly strict. One I found who prohibited the men from all enlivening amusements; I found him sending men to the guard-house for the most trifling offense. In general, perhaps, the officials—especially the new ones, with their straps or badges—put on too many airs. Of all places in the world, the hospitals of American young men and soldiers, wounded in the volunteer service of their country, ought to be exempt from mere conventional military airs and etiquette of shoulder-straps. But they are not exempt.

35

The work of the Army Hospital Visitor is indeed a trade, an art, requiring both experience and natural gifts, and the greatest judgment. A large number of the visitors go from curiosity—as to a show of animals. Others give the men improper things. Then there are always some poor fellows in the cases of sickness or wounds, that imperatively need perfect quiet—not to be talked to by strangers. Few realize that it is not the mere giving of gifts that does good: it is the proper adaptation. Nothing is of any avail among the soldiers except conscientious personal investigation of cases, each one for itself; with sharp, critical faculties, but in the fullest spirit of human sympathy and boundless love.

36

To many of the wounded and sick, especially the youngsters, there is something in personal love, caresses and the magnetic flood of sympathy and friendship, that does, in its way, more good than all the medicine in the world.

37

...in Ward 6, Campbell Hospital—a young man from Plymouth County, Massachusetts; a farmer's son, aged about 20 or 21, a soldierly American young fellow, but with sensitive and tender feelings. Most of December and January last, he lay very low, and for quite a while I never expected he would recover. He had become prostrated with an obstinate diarrhoea; his stomach would hardly keep the least thing down, he was vomiting half the time. But that was hardly the worst of it. Let me tell his story—it is but one of thousands.

He had been some time sick with his regiment in the field, in front, but did his duty as long as he could—was in the battle of

Fredericksburgh—soon after was put in the regimental hospital. He kept getting worse—could not eat anything they had there—the doctor told him nothing could be done for him there—the poor fellow had fever also—received (perhaps it could not be helped) little or no attention—lay on the ground getting worse. Toward the latter part of December, very much enfeebled, he was sent up from the front, from Falmouth Station, in an open platform car; (such as hogs are transported upon north,) and dumped with a crowd of others on the boat at Aquia Creek, falling down like a rag where they deposited him, too weak and sick to sit up or help himself at all. No one spoke to him or assisted him—he had nothing to eat or drink—was used (amid the great crowds of sick) either with perfect indifference, or, as in two or three instances, with heartless brutality.

On the boat, when night came and the air grew chilly, he tried a long time to undo the blankets he had in his knapsack, but was too feeble. He asked one of the employees, who was moving around deck, for a moment's assistance, to get the blankets. The man asked him back if he could not get them himself? He answered no, he had been trying for more than half an hour, and found himself too weak. The man rejoined, he might then go without them, and walked off. So H. lay chill and damp, on deck, all night, without anything under or over him, while two good blankets were within reach. It caused him a great injury—nearly cost him his life.

Arrived at Washington, he was brought ashore and again left on the wharf, or above it, amid the great crowds, as before, without any nourishment—not a drink for his parched mouth—no kind hand offered to cover his face from the forenoon sun. Conveyed at last some two miles by the ambulance to the hospital, and assigned a bed,... he fell down exhausted upon the bed; but the Ward-master (he has since been changed) came to him with a growling order to get up—the rules, he said, permitted no man to lie down in that way with his old clothes on; he must sit up—must first go to the bath-room, be washed, and have his clothes completely changed. (A very good rule, properly applied.) He was taken to the bath-room and scrubbed well with cold water. The attendants, callous for a while, were soon alarmed, for suddenly the half-frozen and lifeless body fell limpsy in their hands, and they hurried it back to the cot, plainly insensible, perhaps dying.

Poor boy! the long train of exhaustion, deprivation, rudeness, no food, no friendly word or deed, but all kinds of upstart airs and impudent, unfeeling speeches and deeds, from all kinds of small officials, (and some big ones,) cutting like razors into that sensitive heart, had at last done the job. He now lay, at times out of his head but quite silent, asking nothing of any one, for some days, with death getting a closer and surer grip upon him—he cared not, or rather he welcomed death. His heart was broken. He felt the struggle to keep up any longer to be useless. God, the world, humanity—all had abandoned him. It would feel so good to shut his eyes forever on the cruel things around him and toward him.

As luck would have it, at this time, I found him. I was passing down Ward No. 6 one day, about dusk (4th of January, I think,) and noticed his glassy eyes, with a look of despair and hopelessness, sunk low in his thin, pallid-brown young face. One learns to divine quickly in the hospital, and as I stopped by him and spoke some commonplace remark, (to which he made no reply,) I saw as I looked that it was a case for ministering to the affection first, and other nourishment and medicines afterward. I sat down by him without any fuss—talked a little—soon saw that it did him good—led him to talk a little himself—got him somewhat interested—wrote a letter for him to his folks in Massachusetts, (to L.H. Campbell, Plymouth County,) soothed him down as I saw he was getting a little too much agitated, and tears in his eyes—gave him some small gifts, and told him I should come again soon. (He has told me since that this little visit, at that hour, just saved him—a day more, and it would have been perhaps too late.)

Of course I did not forget him, for he was a young fellow to interest any one. He remained very sick—vomiting much every day, frequent diarrhoea, and also something like bronchitis, the doctor said. For a while I visited him almost every day—cheered him up—took him some little gifts, and gave him small sums of money, (he relished a drink of new milk, when it was brought through the ward for sale). For a couple of weeks his condition was uncertain—sometimes I

Walt Whitman in 1862

Whitman's brother George, who served throughout the Civil War in an infantry regiment of Brooklyn volunteers.

A farmhouse being used as a hospital. This was the sort of place Whitman saw on his first trip to the front, when he came upon a heap of amputated limbs outside a window.

Aftermath of the shattering battle fought at
Fredericksburg, Virginia, December 1862, in which
George Whitman was wounded.

*Union casualties at a field hospital in northern
Virginia. Whitman saw similar sights during his trip
to the front to find his wounded brother.*

Seven four-wheeled ambulances and their attendants. This kind of vehicle gave wounded men a less painful ride than the see-saw motion of the previously used two-wheeled carts; the canvas-covered sides, which could be rolled up, allowed stretchers to be quickly loaded from both sides.

Abraham Lincoln's manner with people, which Whitman observed on several occasions, and his probity and determination to preserve the Union, moved Whitman to write in one of his wartime memoranda: "I love the President personally."

An open-air field "hospital" at Savage Station, Virginia, after fighting on June 27, 1862, between the Army of the Potomac and the Army of Northern Virginia.

Aftermath of the battle fought at Antietam on September 17, 1862, in which nearly one-third of the troops on both sides were killed or wounded.

Dr. A. Hurd of the 14th Indiana Volunteers moves among makeshift shelters erected on the Antietam battlefield to shade Confederate wounded. Note the hay taken from a nearby farm for bedding and the bayoneted rifles being used to hold up some of the blankets.

thought there was no chance for him at all. But of late he is doing better—is up and dressed, and goes around more and more every day. He will not die, but will recover.

38

When eligible, I encourage the men to write, and myself, when called upon, write all sorts of letters for them, (including love letters, very tender ones.) Almost as I reel off these memoranda, I write for a new patient to his wife. M. de F., of the 17th Connecticut, company H, has just come up (February 17th) from Windmill point, and is received in ward H, Armory-square. He is an intelligent looking man, has a foreign accent, black-eyed and hair'd, a Hebraic appearance. Wants a telegraphic message to his wife, New Canaan, Conn. I agree to send the message—

39

I have seen Charles Sumner three times—he says ev'ry thing here moves as part of a great machine, and that I must consign myself to the fate of the rest—still [in] an interview I had with him yesterday he talked and acted as though he had life in him, and would exert himself to any reasonable extent for me to get something. Meantime I make about enough to pay my expenses by hacking on the press here, and copying in the paymasters' offices, a couple of hours a day. One thing is favorable here, namely pay, for whatever one does is at a high rate. I have not yet presented my letters to either Seward or Chase—I thought I would get my forces all in a body, and make one concentrated dash, if possible with the personal introduction and presence of some big bug. I like fat old Preston King very much—he is fat as a hogshead, with great hanging chops. The first thing he said to me the other day in the parlor chambers of the Senate, when I sent in for him and he came out, was, "Why, how can I do this thing, or any thing for you—how do I know but you are a Secessionist? You look for all the world like an old Southern planter—a regular Carolina or Virginia planter." I treated him with just as much hauteur as he did me with bluntness—this was the first time—it afterward proved that Charles Sumner had not prepared the way for me, as I supposed, or rather not so strongly as I supposed, and Mr. King had even forgotten it—so I was an entire stranger. But the same day C.S. talked further with Mr. King in the Senate, and the second interview I had with the latter (this forenoon) he has given me a sort of general letter, endorsing me from New York—one envelope is addressed to Secretary Chase, and another to Gen. Meigs, head Quartermaster's dept. Meantime, I am getting better and better acquainted with office-hunting wisdom and Washington peculiarities generally.

40

I distribute tobacco in small plugs, with clay pipes, and so on. I think smoking ought not only to be allowed, but rather encouraged, among the men in every ward. I myself never used a pinch of tobacco in any way, but I am clear that in soldiers' hospitals, in barracks, it would be good for the men and neutralize exhalations.

41

A spell of fine soft weather. I wander about a good deal, sometimes at night under the moon. To-night took a long look at the President's house. The white portico—the palace-like, tall, round columns, spotless as snow—the walls also—the tender and soft moonlight, flooding the pale marble, and making peculiar faint languishing shades, not shadows—everywhere a soft transparent hazy, thin, blue moon-lace, hanging in the air—the brilliant and extra-plentiful clusters of gas, on and around the facade, columns, portico, &c.—everything so white, so marbly pure and dazzling, yet soft—the White House of future poems, and of dreams and dramas, there in the soft and copious moon—the gorgeous front, in the trees, under the lustrous flooding moon, full of reality, full of illusion—the forms of the trees, leafless, silent, in trunk and myriad-angles of branches, under the stars and sky—the White House of the land, and of beauty and night—sentries at the gates, and by the portico, silent, pacing there in blue overcoats—stopping you not at all, but eyeing you with sharp eyes, whichever way you move.

42

One young New York man, with a bright, handsome face, had been lying several months from a most disagreeable wound, receiv'd at Bull Run. A bullet had shot him right through the bladder, hitting him front, low in the belly, and coming out back. He had suffer'd much—the water came out of the wound, by slow but steady quantities, for many weeks—so that he lay almost constantly in a sort of puddle—and there were other disagreeable circumstances.

43

In one case, the wife sat by the side of her husband, his sickness typhoid fever, pretty bad. In another, by the side of her son, a mother— she told me she had seven children, and this was the youngest.

44

In general terms a hospital in and around Washington is a cluster of long one-story wooden buildings for the sick wards, and lots of other edifices and large and small tents. There will be ten or twelve wards grouped together, named A, B, C, &c., or numerically 1, 2, or 3, &c. One of these wards will be a hundred to a hundred and fifty feet long, twenty-five or thirty feet wide, and eighteen or twenty feet high, well-windowed, whitewashed inside and out, and kept very clean. It will contain from sixty to a hundred cots, a row on each side, and a space down the middle.... Nearly all the wards are ornamented with evergreens, cheap pictures, &c.

45

February 23.—I must not let the great hospital at the Patent-office pass away without some mention. A few weeks ago the vast area of the second story of that noblest of Washington buildings was crowded close with rows of sick, badly wounded and dying soldiers. They were placed in three very large apartments.... Two of the immense apartments [were] fill'd with high and ponderous glass cases, crowded with models in miniature of every kind of utensil, machine or invention, it ever enter'd into the mind of man to conceive; and with curiosities and foreign presents. Between these cases [were] lateral openings, perhaps eight feet wide and quite deep, and in these were placed the sick, besides a great long double row of them up and down through the middle of the hall. Many of them were very bad cases, wounds and amputations. Then there was a gallery running above the hall in which there were beds also. It was, indeed, a curious scene, especially at night when lit up. The glass cases, the beds, the forms lying there, the gallery above, and the marble pavement under foot—the suffering, and the fortitude to bear it in various degrees—occasionally, from some, the groan that could not be repress'd—sometimes a poor fellow dying, with emaciated face and glassy eye, the nurse by his side, the doctor also there, but no friend, no relative—such were the sights but lately in the Patent-office. (The wounded have since been removed from there, and it is now vacant again.)

46

I spent several hours in the Capitol the other day. The incredible gorgeousness of some of the rooms, (interior decorations, etc.)—rooms used perhaps but for merely three or four committee meetings in the course of a whole year—is beyond one's flightiest dreams. Costly frescoes of the style of Taylor's saloon in Broadway, only really the best and choicest of their sort, done by imported French and Italian artists.... [But] these days, the state our country is in, and especially filled as I am from top to toe of late with scenes and thoughts of the hospitals,... all the poppy-show goddesses, and all the pretty blue and gold in which the interior Capitol is got up, seem to me out of place beyond anything I could tell—and I get away from it as quick as I can when that kind of thought comes over me.

MARCH

47

With my office-hunting, no special result yet. I cannot give up my Hospitals yet. I never before had my feelings so thoroughly and (so far) permanently absorbed, to the very roots, as by these huge swarms of dear, wounded, sick, dying boys—I get very much attached to some of them, and many of them have come to depend on seeing me, and having me sit by them a few minutes, as if for their lives.

48

Soldiers, soldiers, soldiers, you meet everywhere about the city, often superb-looking men, though invalids dress'd in worn uniforms, and carrying canes or crutches. I often have talks with them, occasionally quite long and interesting. One, for instance, will have been all though the peninsula under McClellan—narrates to me the fights, the marches, the strange, quick changes of that eventful campaign, and gives glimpses of many things untold in any official reports or books or journals. These, indeed, are the things that are genuine and precious.... There hangs something majestic about a man who has borne his part in battles, especially if he is very quiet regarding it when you desire him to unbosom. I am continually lost at the absence of blowing and blowers among these old-young American militaires. I have found some man or other who has been in every battle since the war began, and have talk'd with them about each one in every part of the United States, and many of the engagements on the rivers and harbors too. I find men here from every State in the Union, without exception. (There are more Southerners, especially border State men, in the Union army than is generally supposed.) I now doubt whether one can get a fair idea of what this war practically is, or what genuine America is, and her character, without some such experience as this I am having.

49

I go to the Hospitals about the same as ever—the last week or so, I have been most every night to the Capitol, which has been all lit up—I should never get tired of wandering through the Senate wing at night—it is the most costly, splendid and rich-painted place in its interminable mazes (I wander around and lose myself in them) of corridors and halls, that I ever dreamed of, or thought possible to construct—The great Halls of the H of R and the Senate, are wonderful and brilliant at night—they show best then, (in some respects.) They are probably the most beautiful rooms, [in the] ornamented and gilded style, in the world.

50

Men [in the wards] occupy their time in bead work.

51

The Hospitals still engross a large part of my time and feelings— only I don't remain so long and make such exhausting-like visits, the last week—as I have had a bad humming feeling and deafness, stupor-like at times, in my head, which unfits me for continued exertion. It comes from a bad cold, gathering I think in my head. If it were not that some of the soldiers really depend on me to come, and the doctors tell me it is really necessary, I should suspend my visits for two or three days, at least. Poor boys, you have no idea how they cling to one, and how strong the tie that forms between us. Things here are just the same with me, neither better nor worse—(I feel so engrossed with my soldiers, I do not devote that attention to my office-hunting, which is needed for success.)

52

The south is failing fast in many respects—D'Almeida, the Frenchman,... told me that he was besieged every where down south to sell (for confederate money) any and every thing he had, his clothes, his boots, his haversack, &c &c.... to see what I see so much of, puts one entirely out of conceit of war—still for all that I am not sure but I go in for fighting on—the choice is hard on either part, but to *cave* in the worst—

53

I go now steadily to more or less of [the] Hospitals by day or night— find always the sick and dying soldiers forthwith begin to cling to me in a way that makes a fellow feel funny enough. These Hospitals, so different from all others—these thousands, and tens and twenties of thousands of American young men, badly wounded, all sorts of wounds, operated on, pallid with diarrhea, languishing, dying with fever, pneumonia, &c. open a new world somehow to me, giving closer insights, new things, exploring deeper mines than any yet, showing our humanity, (I sometimes put myself in fancy in the cot, with typhoid, or under the knife,) tried by terrible, fearfulest tests, probed deepest, the living soul's, the body's tragedies, bursting the petty bonds of art. To these, what are your dramas and poems, even the oldest and the tearfulest? Not old Greek mighty ones, where man contends with fate, (and always yields)—not Virgil showing Dante on and on among the agonized & damned, approach what here I see and take a part in. For here I see, not at intervals, but quite always, how certain, man, our American man—how he holds himself cool and unquestioned master above all pains and bloody mutilations. It is immense, the best thing of all, nourishes me of all men.

54

The army wagons without end, the ambulances—the group of offi- cers & perpetual squad of soldiers—the sick crawling around, many with crutches, the pallid faces & slow weak step—the procession of rebel prisoners, all ragged & dirty, as a huge raff, yet through the dirt & rags the American face & form, strong & clear appears. Under heavy guard they move along, carrying old blankets, quilts, their heads held high. No remarks from the crowd.—I have seen them often, yet never heard one sign of jeer or offensive exultation—the wounds, the shoeless, some without hats, rags around their heads.

55

—there is among the Old Capitol prisoners a little boy of seven years old—he and his father were taken as secesh guerillas in Virginia, and the government is holding on to the child, to exchange him for some Union prisoner south.... My heart bleeds at all sorts of such damnable things of one kind or another I meet with every day—it is not the fault of the President—he would not harm any human being—nor of Seward or Stanton—but the heartless mean-souled brutes that get in positions subordinate but where they can show themselves, and their damned airs and pomposity—they think nothing of treating a man like the worst slave-owner is supposed to treat his niggers—

56

—have struck up a tremendous friendship with a young Mississippi captain (about 19) that we took prisoner badly wounded at Fredericksburg—he has followed me here, is in Emory hospital here, minus a leg—he wears his confederate uniform, proud as the devil—I met him first at Falmouth, in the Lacy house, middle of December last, his leg just cut off, and cheered him up—poor boy, he has suffered a great deal, and still suffers—has eyes bright as a hawk, but face pale—our affection is quite an affair, quite romantic—sometimes when I lean over to say I am going, he puts his arm round my neck, draws my face down, &c.

57

Washington and its points I find bear a second and a third perusal, and doubtless indeed many.... Upon the whole, the city, the spaces, buildings, &c make no unfit emblem of our country, so far, so broadly planned, every thing in plenty, money & materials staggering with plenty, but the fruit of the plans, the knit, the combination yet wanting—Determined to express ourselves greatly in a capital but no fit capital yet here—(time, associations, wanting, I suppose)—many a hiatus yet—many a thing to be taken down and done over again yet—perhaps an entire change of base—may-be a succession of changes. Congress does not seize very hard upon me—I studied it and its members with curiosity, and long—much gab, great fear of public opinion, plenty of low business talent, but no masterful man in Congress, (probably best so.) I think well of the President. He has a face like a hoosier Michael Angelo, so awful ugly it becomes beautiful, with its strange mouth, its deep cut, criss-cross lines, and its doughnut complexion. My notion is, too, that underneath his outside smutched mannerism, and stories from third-class county bar-rooms, (it is his humor,) Mr. Lincoln keeps a fountain of first-class practical telling wisdom. I do not dwell on the supposed failures of his government; he has shown, I sometimes think, an almost supernatural tact in keeping the ship afloat at all, with head steady, not only not going down, and now certain not to, but with proud and resolute spirit, and flag flying in sight of the world, menacing and high as ever. I say never yet captain, never ruler, had such a perplexing, dangerous task as his, the past two years. I more and more rely upon his idiomatic western genius, careless of court dress or court decorums.

58

I am living here without much definite aim, (except going to the hospitals)—yet I have quite a good time—I make some money by scribbling for the papers, and as copyist. I have had, (and have,) thoughts of trying to get a clerkship or something, but I only try in a listless sort of way, and of course do not succeed. I have strong letters of introduction from Mr. Emerson to Mr. Seward and Mr. Chase, but I have not presented them. I have seen Mr. Sumner several times anent of my office-hunting—he promised fair once—but he does not seem to be finally fascinated. I hire a bright little 3d story front room, with service, &c. for $7 a month, dine in the same house, (394 L st. a private house)—and remain yet much of the old vagabond that so gracefully becomes me…. My beard, neck, &c. are woolier, fleecier, whiteyer than ever. I wear army boots, with magnificent black morocco tops, the trousers put in, wherein shod and legged confront I Virginia's deepest mud with supercilious eyes. The scenery around Washington is really fine, the Potomac a lordly river, the hills, woods, &c all attractive. I poke about quite a good deal. Much of the weather here is from heaven—of late, though, a stretch decidedly from the other point. To-night (for it is night, about 10) I sit alone writing this.... A gentleman and his wife, who occupy the two other apartments on this floor, have gone to see Heron in Medea—have put their little child to bed, and left me in charge. The little one is sleeping soundly there in the back room, and I, (plagued with a cold in the head,) sit here in the front, by a good fire, writing as aforesaid.... The evening is lonesome & still.

59

This is a large building, filled with paymasters' offices, some thirty or forty or more. This room is up on the fifth floor, (a most noble and broad view from my window.) Curious scenes around here—a continual stream of soldiers, officers, cripples, &c &c. some climbing wearily up the stairs. They seek their pay—and every hour, almost every minute, has its incident, its hitch, its romance, farce or tragedy. There are two paymasters in this room. A sentry at the street door, another half way up the stairs, another at the chief clerk's door, all with muskets & bayonets—sometimes a great swarm, hundreds, around the side walk in front, waiting. (Every body is waiting for something here.) I take a pause, look up a couple of minutes from my pen and paper—see spread, off there, the Potomac, very fine, nothing petty about it—the Washington monument, not half finished—the public grounds around it filled with ten thousand beeves, on the hoof—to the left the Smithsonian with its brown turrets—to the right, far across, Arlington Heights, the forts, eight or ten of them—then the long bridge, and down a ways, but quite plain, the shipping of Alexandria—opposite me, and in stone throw, is the Treasury building—and below the bustle and life of Pennsylvania avenue.

60

...it is quite a snow-storm here this morning—the ground is an inch and a half deep with snow—and it is snowing and drizzling—but I feel very independent in my stout army-boots; I go anywhere.

APRIL

61

This country can't be broken up by Jeff Davis, & all his damned crew.... I sometimes feel as if I didn't want to live—life would have no charm for me, if this country should fail after all, and be reduced to take a third rate position, to be domineered over by England & France & the haughty nations of Europe &c and we unable to help ourselves. But I have no thought that will ever be, this country I hope would spend her last drop of blood, and last dollar, rather than submit to such humiliation.

62

—I believe I weigh about 200, and as to my face, (so scarlet,) and my beard and neck, they are terrible to behold. I fancy the reason I am able to do some good in the hospitals among the poor languishing and wounded boys, is, that I am so large and well—indeed like a great wild buffalo, with much hair. Many of the soldiers are from the West, and far North, and they take to a man that has not the bleached shiny and shaved cut of the cities and the East.

63

Diseases of the throat and bronchia are the result always of bad state of the stomach, blood, etc. (they never come from the throat itself). The throat and the bronchia are lined, like the stomach and other interior organs, with a fine lining like silk or crape, and when all this gets ulcerated or inflamed or whatnot... it is bad, and most distressing. Medicine is really of no great account, except just to pacify a person. This lining I speak of is full of little blood vessels, and the way to make a *real cure* is by gentle and steady means to recuperate the whole system; this will tell upon the blood, upon the blood vessels, and so finally and effectually upon all this coating I speak of that lines the throat, etc.

64

Every now and then, in hospital or camp, there are beings I meet—specimens of unworldliness, disinterestedness, and animal purity and heroism—perhaps some unconscious Indianian, or from Ohio or Tennessee—on whose birth the calmness of heaven seems to have descended, and whose gradual growing up, whatever the circumstances of work-life or change, or hardship, or small or no education that attended it, the power of a strange spiritual sweetness, fibre and inward health, have also attended. Something veil'd and abstracted is often a part of the manners of these beings. I have met them, I say, not seldom in the army, in camp, and in the hospitals. The Western regiments contain many of them. They are often young men, obeying the events and occasions about them, marching, soldiering, fighting, foraging, cooking, working on farms or at some trade before the war—unaware of their own nature, (as to that, who is aware of his own nature?) their companions only understanding that they are different from the rest, more silent, "something odd about them," and apt to go off and meditate and muse in solitude.

65

I spent three to four hours yesterday in Armory hospital. One of my particular boys there was dying—pneumonia—he wanted me to stop with him awhile; he could not articulate—but the look of his eyes, and the holding on of his hand was deeply affecting. His case is a relapse—eight days ago he had recovered, was up, was perhaps a little careless—at any rate took cold, was taken down again and has sunk rapidly. He has no friends or relatives here.

It don't seem to me it makes so much difference about worldly successes (beyond just enough to eat and drink and shelter, in the moderatest limits) any more, since the last four months of my life especially, and that merely to live, and have one fair meal a day, is enough—

MAY

67

Saw the procession of rebel prisoners (about 100) march down Pennsylvania Ave. under guard, to the Old Capitol Prison. We talk brave & get excited & indignant over the "rebels," & drink perdition to them—but I realized how all anger sinks into nothing in sight of these young men & standing close by them & seeing them pass. They were wretchedly drest, very dirty & worthless in rig, but generally bright good looking fellows—I felt that they were by brothers, just about the same as the rest—I felt my heart full of compassion & brotherhood, & the irrepressible absurd tears started in my eyes,— these too are my brothers—it was in the look of them & in my heart—the common people these, American, silent proud young fellows—(there was not one single expression of insult or comment from the crowd, along Pennsylvania Avenue—not the slightest—the prisoners were surrounded with a cordon of guards with loaded muskets)—to have suffered! what a title it gives!—

68

—As I write this, the wounded have begun to arrive from Hooker's command from bloody Chancellorsville. I was down among the first arrivals. The men in charge told me the bad cases were yet to come. If that is so I pity them, for these are bad enough. You ought to see the scene of the wounded arriving at the landing here at the foot of

Sixth street, at night. Two boat loads came about half-past seven last night. A little after eight it rain'd a long and violent shower. The pale, helpless soldiers had been debark'd, and lay around on the wharf and neighborhood anywhere. The rain was, probably, grateful to them; at any rate they were exposed to it. The few torches light up the spectacle. All around—on the wharf, on the ground, out on side places— the men are lying on blankets, old quilts, &c., with bloody rags bound round heads, arms, and legs. The attendants are few, and at night few outsiders also—only a few hard-work'd transportation men and drivers. (The wounded are getting to be common, and people grow callous.) The men, whatever their condition, lie there, and patiently wait till their turn comes to be taken up. Near by, the ambulances are now arriving in clusters, and one after another is call'd to back up and take its load.

69

...timely contributions from D. L. Northrup, John H. Rhodes, Thos. Cotrel, Nicholas Wyckoff, & Thomas Sullivan, for my poor men here in the hospital. With these, as with other funds, I aid all I can soldiers from all the states... —it is a work of God's charity, never cases more deserving of aid, never more heart-rending cases, than these now coming up in one long bloody string from Chancellorsville and Fredericksburgh battles, six or seven hundred every day without intermission. We have already over 3000 arrived here in hospital from Hooker's late battles. I work somewhere among them every day or in the evening.

70

...the Rebellion has lost worse and more than we have. The more I find out about it, the more I think they, the Confederates, have received an irreparable harm and loss in Virginia—I should not be surprised to see them (either voluntarily or by force) leaving Virginia before many weeks; I don't see how on earth they can stay there.

—my poor, poor boys occupy my time very much—I go every day, and sometimes nights... a young man in Ward F, Armory-square, with a bad wound in the leg, very agonizing—had to have it propt up, and an attendant all the while dripping water on night and day. I was in hopes at one time he would get through with it, but a few days ago he took a sudden bad turn and died about 3 o'clock the same afternoon—it was horrible. He was of good family—handsome, intelligent man, about 26, married; his name was John Elliot, of Cumberland Valley, Bedford co., Penn.—belonged to 2nd Pennsylvania Cavalry. I felt very bad about it. I have wrote to his father—have not received any answer yet; no friend nor any of his folks was here, and have not been here nor sent—probably don't know of it at all. The surgeons put off amputating the leg, he was so exhausted, but at last it was imperatively necessary to amputate.... He never came alive off the amputating table—he died under the operation—it was what I had dreaded and anticipated. Poor young man, he suffered much, very, *very* much, for many days, and bore it so patiently—so that it was a release to him.... Such things are awful—not a soul here he knew or cared about, except me—yet the surgeons and nurses were good to him. I think all was done for him that could be—there was no help but take off the leg; he was under chloroform—they tried their best to bring him to—three long hours were spent, a strong smelling bottle held under his nostrils, with other means, three hours.... How contemptible all the usual little worldly prides and vanities, and striving after appearances, seems in the midst of such scenes as these—such tragedies of soul and body. To see such things and not be able to help them is awful—I feel almost ashamed of being so well and whole.

72

[The Battle of Chancellorsville] was largely in the woods, and quite a general engagement. The night was very pleasant, at times the moon shining out full and clear, all Nature so calm in itself, the early summer grass so rich, and foliage of the trees—yet there the battle raging, and many good fellows lying helpless, with new accessions to them, and every minute amid the rattle of muskets and crash of cannon, (for there was an artillery contest too,) the red life-blood oozing out from heads or trunks or limbs upon that green and dew-cool grass. Patches of the woods take fire, and several of the wounded, unable to move, are consumed—quite large spaces are swept over, burning the dead also—some of the men have their hair and beard singed—some, burns on their faces and hands—others holes burnt in their clothing. The flashes of fire from the cannon, the quick flaring flames and smoke, and the immense roar—the musketry so general, the light nearly bright enough for each side to see the other—the crashing, tramping of men—the yelling—close quarters—we hear the secesh yells—our men cheer loudly back, especially if Hooker is in sight—hand to hand conflicts, each side stands up to it, brave, determin'd as demons, they often charge upon us—a thousand deeds are done worth to write newer greater poems on—and still the woods on fire—still many are not only scorch'd—too many, unable to move, are burn'd to death.

73

...it is all a lottery, this war; no one knows what will come up next.

74

—I often go [to the wards], just at dark, sometimes stay nearly all night—I like to go just before supper, carrying a pot or jar of something good & go around with a spoon distributing a little here and there. Yet after all this succoring of the stomach (which is of course most welcome and indispensable) I should say that I believe my profoundest help to these sick & dying men is probably the soothing invigoration I steadily bear in mind, to infuse in them through affection, cheering love, & the like, between them & me. It has saved more than one life. There is a strange influence here. I have formed attachments here in hospital, that I shall keep to my dying day, & they will the same, without doubt.

75

In my visits to the hospitals I found it was in the simple matter of personal presence, and emanating ordinary cheer and magnetism, that I succeeded and help'd more than by medical nursing, or delicacies, or gifts of money, or anything else.... My habit, when practicable, was to prepare for starting out on one of those daily or nightly tours of from a couple to four or five hours, by fortifying myself with previous rest, the bath, clean clothes, a good meal, and as cheerful an appearance as possible.

76

...I have discarded my old clothes—somewhat because they were too thick, and more still because they were worse gone in than any I have ever yet wore, I think, in my life, especially in the trowsers. Wearing my big boots had caused the inside of the legs just above the knee to wear two beautiful round holes right through cloth and partly through the lining, producing a novel effect, which was not necessary, as I produce a sufficient sensation without—then they were desperately faded. I have a nice plain suit of a dark wine color; looks very well, and feels good—single breasted sack coat with breast pockets, etc., and vest and pants same as what I always wear (pants pretty full), so upon the whole all looks unusually good for me. My hat is very good yet, boots ditto; have a new necktie, nice shirts—... I cut quite a swell. I have not trimmed my beard since I left home, but it is not grown much longer, only perhaps a little bushier. I keep about as stout as ever, and the past five or six days I have felt wonderful well, indeed never did I feel better.

77

The soldiers are nearly all young men, and far more American than is generally supposed—I should say nine-tenths are native-born. Among the arrivals from Chancellorsville I find a large proportion of Ohio, Indiana, and Illinois men. As usual, there are all sorts of wounds. Some of the men fearfully burnt from the explosions of artillery caissons. One ward has a long row of officers, some with ugly hurts. Yesterday was perhaps worse than usual. Amputations are going on—the attendants are dressing wounds As you pass by, you must be on your guard where you look. I saw the other day a gentleman, a visitor apparently from curiosity, in one of the wards, stop and turn a moment to look at an awful wound they were probing. He turn'd pale, and in a moment more he had fainted away and fallen on the floor.

78

I saw the lieutenant when he was first brought here from Chancellorsville, and have been with him occasionally from day to day and night to night. He had been getting along pretty well till night before last, when a sudden hemorrhage that could not be stopt came upon him, and to-day it still continues at intervals. Notice that water-pail by the side of the bed, with a quantity of blood and bloody pieces of muslin, nearly full; that tells the story. The poor young man is struggling painfully for breath, his great dark eyes with a glaze already upon them, and the choking faint but audible in his throat. An attendant sits by him, and will not leave him till the last; yet little or nothing can be done. He will die here in an hour or two, without the presence of kith or kin. Meantime the ordinary chat and business of the ward a little way off goes on indifferently. Some of the inmates are laughing and joking, others are playing checkers or cards, others are reading, &c.

79

Opposite, an old Quaker lady is sitting by the side of her son, Amer Moore, 2d U.S. artillery—shot in the head two weeks since, very low, quite rational—from hips down paralyzed—he will surely die. I speak a very few words to him every day and evening—he answers pleasantly—wants nothing—(he told me soon after he came about his home affairs, his mother had been an invalid, and he fear'd to let her know his condition.)

80

—most everybody here carries an umbrella, on account of the sun. Yesterday and to-day however have been quite cool, east wind.

81

Do not be discouraged. I am not even here—here amid all this huge mess of traitors, loafers, hospitals, axe-grinders, & incompetencies & officials that goes by the name of Washington.

JUNE

82

—Great as the Army Hospitals already are, they are rapidly growing greater and greater. I have heard that the number of our army sick regularly under treatment now exceeds three hundred and fifty thousand.

83

...the war still goes on, and everything as much in a fog as ever—and the battles as bloody, and the wounded and sick getting worse and plentier all the time.

84

We have strawberries good and plenty, 15 cents a quart, with the hulls on—I go down to market sometimes of a morning and buy two or three quarts, for the folks I take my meals with. ... I have not paid, as you may say, a cent of board since I have been in Washington, that is for meals—four or five times I have made a rush to leave the folks and find a moderate-priced boarding-house, but every time they have made such a time about it that I have kept on. It is Mr. and Mrs. O'Connor (he is the author of "Harrington"); he has a $1600 office in the Treasury, and she is a first-rate woman, a Massachusetts girl.

...I think something of commencing a series of lectures and readings, etc., through different cities of the north, to supply myself with funds for my Hospital and Soldiers visits—as I do not like to be beholden to the medium of others. I need a pretty large supply of money, etc., to do the good I would like to, and the work grows upon me, and fascinates me—it is the most affecting thing you ever see, the lots of poor sick and wounded young men that depend so much, in one word or another, upon my petting or soothing or feeding, sitting by them and feeding them their dinner or supper—some are quite helpless, some wounded in both arms—or giving some trifle (for a novelty or a change, it isn't for the value of it), or stopping a little while with them. Nobody will do but me—so... I feel as though I would like to inaugurate a plan by which I could raise means on my own hook, and perhaps quite plenty too.

86

June 18th.—In one of the hospitals I find Thomas Haley, company M, 4th New York cavalry—a regular Irish boy, a fine specimen of youthful physical manliness—shot through the lungs—inevitably dying—came over to this country from Ireland to enlist—has not a single friend or acquaintance here—is sleeping soundly at this moment, (but it is the sleep of death)—has a bullet-hole straight through the lung. I saw Tom when first brought here, three days since, and didn't suppose he could live twelve hours—(yet he looks well enough in the face to a casual observer.)

87

I have not missed a day at hospital, I think, for more than three weeks—I get more and more wound round. Poor young men—there are some cases that would literally sink and give up if I did not pass a portion of the time with them.

Office Christian Commission,

No. 13 Bank Street.

Philadelphia, *Jany 20th 1863*

To Officers of the Army and Navy of the United States, and others:

The **CHRISTIAN COMMISSION,** organized by a Convention of the Young Men's Christian Associations of the loyal States, to promote the spiritual and temporal welfare and improvement of the men of the Army and Navy, acting under the approbation and commendation of the President, the Secretaries of the Army and the Navy, and of the Generals in command, have appointed

Walt Whitman of Brooklyn N.Y.

A Delegate, to act in accordance with instructions furnished herewith, under direction of the proper officers, in furtherance of the objects of the Christian Commission.

His services will be rendered in behalf of the Christian Commission, without remuneration from, or expense to, the Government.

His work will be that of distributing stores where needed, in hospitals and camps; circulating good reading matter amongst soldiers and sailors; visiting the sick and wounded, to instruct, comfort and cheer them, and aid them in correspondence with their friends at home; aiding Surgeons on the battle-field and elsewhere in the care and conveyance of the wounded to hospitals; helping Chaplains in their ministrations and influence for the good of the men under their care ; and addressing soldiers and sailors, individually and collectively, in explanation of the work of the Christian Commission and its Delegates, and for their personal instruction and benefit, temporal and eternal.

All possible facilities, and all due courtesies, are asked for him, in the proper pursuance of any or all of these duties.

Geo, H. Stuart

Chairman Christian Commission.

Whitman obtained this certificate from the Christian Commission to allow him free travel between Washington and Brooklyn. He praised the work of this private organization, but criticized the government-created Sanitary Commission in its care of sick and wounded soldiers.

88

...we are generally anticipating a lively time here, or in the neighborhood, as it is probably Lee is feeling about to strike a blow on Washington, or perhaps right into it—and as Lee is no fool, it is perhaps possible he may give us a good shake. He is not very far off—yesterday was a fight to the southwest of here all day; we heard the cannons nearly all day.

89

As to the Sanitary commissions and the like, I am sick of them all, and would not accept any of their berths. You ought to see the way the men, as they lay helpless in bed, turn away their faces from the sight of those agents, chaplains, etc. (hirelings, as Elias Hicks would call them—they seem to me always a set of foxes and wolves). They get well paid, and are always incompetent and disagreeable... the only good fellows I have met are the Christian commissioners—they go everywhere and receive no pay.

90

In this same hospital, Armory-square, where [the] cavalry boy is, I have about fifteen or twenty particular cases I see much to—some of them as much as him. There are two from East Brooklyn: George Monk, Co. A, 78th N.Y., and Stephen Redgate (his mother is a widow in East Brooklyn—I have written to her). Both are pretty badly wounded—both are youngsters under 19.... It seems to me as I go through these rows of cots as if it was too bad to accept these *children*, to subject them to such premature experiences. I devote myself much to Armory-square hospital because it contains by far the worst cases, most repulsive wounds, has the most suffering and most need of consolation. I go every day without fail, and often at night—sometimes stay very late. No one interferes with me, guards, nurses, doctors, nor anyone. I am let to take my own course.

One soldier brought here about fifteen days ago, very low with typhoid fever, Livingston Brooks, Co. B., 17th Penn. Cavalry, I have particularly stuck to, as I found him to be in what appeared to be a dying condition, from negligence and a horrible journey of about forty miles, bad roads and fast driving; and then after he got here, as he is a simple country boy, very shy and silent, and made no complaint, they neglected him. I found him something like I found John Holmes last winter. I called the doctor's attention to him, shook up the nurses, had him bathed in spirits, gave him lumps of ice, and ice to head; he had a fearful bursting pain in his head, and his body was like fire. He was very quiet, a very sensible boy, old fashioned; he did not want to die, and I had to lie to him without stint, for he thought he knew everything, and I always put in of course that what I told him was exactly the truth, and that if he got really dangerous I would tell him and not conceal it. The rule is to remove bad fever patients out from the main wards to a tent by themselves, and the doctor told me he would have to be removed. I broke it gently to him, but the poor boy got it immediately in his head that he was marked with death, and was to be removed on that account. It had a great effect upon him, and although I told the truth this time it did not have as good a result as my former fibs. I persuaded the doctor to let him remain. For three days he lay just about an even chance, go or stay, with a little leaning toward the first. But... he is now out of any immediate danger. He has been perfectly rational throughout—begins to taste a little food (for a week he ate nothing; I had to compel him to take a quarter of an orange now and then), and I will say, whether anyone calls it pride or not, that if he *does* get up and around again it's me that saved his life.

The Reb cavalry come quite near us, dash in and steal wagon trains, etc.; it would be funny if they should come some night to the President's country house (Soldier's home), where he goes out to sleep every night; it is in the same direction as their saucy raid last Sunday.

Mr. Lincoln passes here (14th st.) every evening on his way out.... I really think it would be safer for him just now to stop at the White House, but I expect he is too proud to abandon the former custom. Then about an hour after, we had a large cavalry regiment pass, with blankets, arms, etc., on the war march over the same track. The regt. was very full, over a thousand— ...They were preceded by a fine mounted band of sixteen (about ten bugles, the rest cymbals and drums).... It made everything ring—made my heart leap. They played with a will. Then the accompaniment: the sabers rattled on a thousand men's sides—they had pistols, their heels were spurred— handsome American young men (I make no acc't of any other); rude uniforms, well worn, but good cattle, prancing—all good riders, full of the devil; nobody shaved, very sunburnt. The regimental officers (splendidly mounted, but just as roughly dressed as the men) came immediately after the band, then company after company, with each its officers at its head—the tramps of so many horses (there is a good hard turnpike)—then a long train of men with led horses, mounted negroes, and a long, long string of baggage wagons, each with four horses, and then a strong rear guard. I tell you it had the look of *real war*—noble looking fellows; a man feels so proud on a good horse, and armed. They are off toward the region of Lee's (supposed) rendezvous, toward Susquehannah, for the great anticipated battle. Alas! how many of these healthy, handsome, rollicking young men will lie cold in death before the apples ripen in the orchard.

93

There are getting to be *many black troops.* There is one very good regt. here black as tar; they go around, have the regular uniform—they submit to no nonsense. Others are constantly forming. It is getting to be a common sight.

94

—This forenoon, for more than an hour, again long strings of cavalry, several regiments, very fine men and horses, four or five abreast. I saw then in Fourteenth street, coming in town from north. Several hundred extra horses, some of the mares with colts, trotting along… just as they had all pass'd, a string of ambulances commenc'd from the other way, moving up Fourteenth street north, slowly wending along, bearing a large lot of wounded to the hospitals.

95

July 4th.—The weather to-day, upon the whole, is very fine, warm, but from a smart rain last night, fresh enough, and no dust, which is a great relief for this city. I saw the parade about noon, Pennsylvania avenue, from Fifteenth street down toward the capitol. There were three regiments of infantry, (I suppose the ones doing patrol duty here,) two or three societies of Odd Fellows, a lot of children in barouches, and a squad of policemen. (A useless imposition upon the soldiers—they have work enough on their backs without piling the like of this.) As I went down the Avenue, saw a big flaring placard on the bulletin board of a newspaper office, announcing "Glorious Victory for the Union Army!" Meade had fought Lee at Gettysburg, Pennsylvania, yesterday and day before, and repuls'd him most signally, taken 3,000 prisoners, &c. (I afterwards saw Meade's despatch, very modest, and a sort of order of the day from the President himself, quite religious, giving thanks to the Supreme, and calling on the people to do the same.) I walk'd on to Armory hospital—took along with me several bottles of blackberry and cherry syrup, good and strong, but innocent. Went through several of the wards, announc'd to the soldiers the news from Meade, and gave them all a good drink of the syrups with ice water, quite refreshing—prepar'd it all myself, and serv'd it around. Meanwhile the Washington bells are ringing their sundown peals for Fourth of July, and the usual fusilades of boys' pistols, crackers, and guns.

July 6th.—A steady rain, dark and thick and warm. A train of six-mule wagons has just pass'd bearing pontoons, great square-end flat-boats, and the heavy planking for overlaying them. We hear that the Potomac above here is flooded, and are wondering whether Lee will be able to get back across again, or whether Meade will indeed break him to pieces.

97

Washington, Wednesday forenoon, July 15, 1863… —So the mob has risen at last in New York—I have been expecting it, but as the day for the draft had arrived and everything was so quiet, I supposed all might go on smoothly; but it seems the passions of the people were only sleeping, and have burst forth with terrible fury, and they have destroyed life and property, the enrollment buildings, etc., as we hear. The accounts we get are a good deal in a muddle, but it seems bad enough. The feeling here is savage and hot as fire against New York (the mob—"Copperhead mob" the papers here call it), and I hear nothing in all directions but threats of ordering up the gun-boats, cannonading the city, shooting down the mob, hanging them in a body, etc., etc. Meantime I remain silent, partly amused, partly scornful, or occasionally put a dry remark which only adds fuel to the flame. I do not feel it in my heart to abuse the poor people, or call for a rope or bullets for them, but that is all the talk here, even in the hospitals. The acc'ts from N.Y. this morning are that the Gov't has ordered the draft to be suspended there—I hope it is true, for I find that the deeper they go in with the draft, the more trouble it is likely to make.

98

They have the men wounded in the railroad accident at Laurel station (between here and Baltimore), about 30 soldiers, some of them horribly injured at 3 o'clock A.M. last Saturday by collision—poor, poor, poor men. I go again this afternoon and night—I see so much of butcher sights, so much sickness and suffering, I must get away a while, I believe, for self-preservation.

99

This afternoon, July 22d, I have spent a long time with Oscar F. Wilber, company G, 154th New York, low with chronic diarrhoea, and a bad wound also. He asked me to read him a chapter in the New Testament. I complied, and ask'd him what I should read. He said, "Make your own choice." I open'd at the close of one of the first books of the evangelists, and read the chapters describing the latter hours of Christ, and the scenes at the crucifixion. The poor, wasted young man ask'd me to read the following chapter also, how Christ rose again. I read very slowly, for Oscar was feeble. It pleased him very much, yet the tears were in his eyes. He ask'd me if I enjoy'd religion. I said, "Perhaps not, my dear, in the way you mean, and yet, may-be, it is the same thing." He said, "It is my chief reliance." He talk'd of death, and said he did not fear it. I said, "Why, Oscar, don't you think you will get well?" He said, "I may, but it is not probable." He spoke calmly of his condition. The wound was very bad, it discharg'd much. Then the diarrhoea had prostrated him, and I felt that he was even then the same as dying. He behaved very manly and affectionate. The kiss I gave him as I was about leaving he return'd fourfold. He gave me his mother's address, Mrs. Sally D. Wilber, Alleghany post-office, Cattaraugus county, N.Y. I had several such interviews with him. He died a few days after the one just described.

100

[*letter to parents of a hospitalized soldier*]

Washington   July 27, 1863

Mr and Mrs Haskell
    Your son Erastus Haskell, of Co K 141st New York, is now lying sick with typhoid fever here in hospital.

I have been with him quite a good deal, from day to day, was with him yesterday & indeed almost every day, & feel much interested in the young man. He has been very sick, & seems to be so now, as I should judge, but the doctor says he will recover. I had a talk with the doctor yesterday, & he says so still. But Erastus seems to me very sick, & I thought I would write to you. He had some one write to you about two weeks ago, but has received no answer.

Erastus does not talk much, so I do not understand much about his affairs. I am merely a friend. The address of Erastus is

Ward E, Armory Square Hospital
Washington D C

should you wish to write him direct.

Walt Whitman
care Major Hapgood, paymaster
U S A cor 15th & F st
Washington
D C

Upon second thought I enclose you an envelope to send your letter to Erastus—put a stamp on it, & write soon. I suppose you know he has been sick a great deal since he has been in the service.

AUGUST

101

O what a sweet unwonted love (those good American boys, of good stock, decent, clean, well raised boys, so near to me)—what an attachment grows up between us, started from hospital cots, where pale young faces lie & wounded or sick bodies. My brave young American soldiers—now for so many months I have gone around among them, where they lie. I have long discarded all stiff conventions (they & I are too near to each other, there is no time to lose, &

death & anguish dissipate ceremony here between my lads & me)—
I pet them, some of them it does so much good, they are so faint &
lonesome—at parting at night sometimes I kiss them right & left—
The doctors tell me I supply the patients with a medicine which all
their drugs & bottles & powders are helpless to yield.

102

[*another letter to the same parents*]

Washington   August 10 1863

Mr and Mrs Haskell,
    Dear friends, I thought it would be soothing to you to have a few
lines about the last days of your son Erastus Haskell of Company K,
141st New York Volunteers. I write in haste, & nothing of importance—only I thought any thing about Erastus would be welcome.
From the time he came to Armory Square Hospital till he died, there
was hardly a day but I was with him a portion of the time—if not
during the day, then at night. I had no opportunity to do much, or
any thing for him, as nothing was needed, only to wait the progress
of his malady. I am only a friend, visiting the wounded & sick soldiers, (not connected with any society—or State.) From the first I
felt that Erastus was in danger, or at least was much worse than they
in the hospital supposed....
    I was very anxious he should be saved, & so were they all—he
was well used by the attendants—poor boy, I can see him as I write—
he was tanned & had a fine head of hair, & looked good in the face
when he first came, & was in pretty good flesh too—(had his hair cut
close about ten or twelve days before he died)—He never com-
plained—but it looked pitiful to see him lying there, with such a look
out of his eyes. He had large clear eyes, they seemed to talk better
than words—I assure you I was attracted to him much—Many
nights I sat in the hospital by his bedside till far in the night—The
lights would be put out—yet I would sit there silently, hours, late,
perhaps fanning him—he always liked to have me sit there, but never

cared to talk—I shall never forget those nights, it was a curious & solemn scene, the sick & wounded lying around in their cots, just visible in the darkness, & this dear young man close at hand lying on what proved to be his death bed—I do not know his past life, but what I do know, & what I saw of him, he was a noble boy—I felt he was one I should get very much attached to. I think you have reason to be proud of such a son, & all his relatives have cause to treasure his memory.

I write to you this letter, because I would do something at least in his memory—his fate was a hard one, to die so—He is one of the thousands of our unknown American young men in the ranks about whom there is no record or fame, no fuss made about their dying so unknown, but I find in them the real precious & royal ones of this land, giving themselves, up, aye even their young & precious lives, in their country's cause— …Though we are strangers & shall probably never see each other, I send you & all Erastus' brothers & sisters my love—

Walt Whitman

I live when at home, in Brooklyn, N Y. (in Portland avenue, 4th door north of Myrtle, my mother's residence.) My address here is care of Major Hapgood, paymaster U S A, cor 15th & F st., Washington D C.

103

As time passes on it seems as if sad cases of old & lingering wounded accumulate, regularly recruited with new ones every week—I have been most of this day in Armory Square Hospital, Seventh st. I seldom miss a day or evening. Out of the six or seven hundred in this Hosp I try to give a word or a trifle to every one without exception, making regular rounds among them all. I give all kinds of sustenance, blackberries, peaches, lemons & sugar, wines, all kinds of preserves, pickles, brandy, milk, shirts & all articles of underclothing, tobacco, tea, handkerchiefs, &c &c &c. I always give paper, envelopes, stamps, &c. I want a supply for this purpose. To many I give (when I have it) small sums of money—half of the soldiers in hospital have not a cent. There are many returned prisoners, sick, lost all—& every day squads of men from [the] front, cavalry or infantry—brought in wounded or sick, generally without a cent of money. Then I select the most needy cases & devote my time & services much to them. I find it tells best—some are mere lads, 17, 18, 19, or 20. Some are silent, sick, heavy hearted, (things, attentions, &c. are very rude in the army & hospitals, nothing but the mere hard routine, no time for tenderness or extras)—So I go round—Some of my boys die, some get well—…

I am at present curiously almost alone here, as visitor & consolator to Hospitals—the work of the different Reliefs & Commissions is nearly all off in the field—& as to private visitors, *there are few or none*— …I go among all our own dear soldiers, hospital camps & army, our teamsters' hospitals, among sick & dying, the rebels, the contrabands, &c &c. What I reach is necessarily but a drop in the bucket but it is done in good faith, & with now some experience & I hope with good heart.

104

August 8th.—To-night, as I was trying to keep cool, sitting by a wounded soldier in Armory-square, I was attracted by some pleasant singing in an adjoining ward. As my soldier was asleep, I left him, and entering the ward where the music was, I walk'd half-way down and took a seat by the cot of a young Brooklyn friend, S.R., badly wounded in the hand at Chancellorsville, and who has suffer'd much, but at that moment in the evening was wide awake and comparatively easy. He had turn'd over on his left side to get a better view of the singers, but the mosquito-curtains of the adjoining cots obstructed the sight. I stept round and loop'd them all up, so that he had a clear show, and then sat down again by him, and look'd and listen'd. The principal singer was a young lady-nurse of one of the wards, accompanying on a melodeon, and join'd by the lady-nurses of other wards. They sat there, making a charming group, with their handsome, healthy faces, and standing up a little behind them were some ten or fifteen of the convalescent soldiers, young men, nurses, &c., with books in their hands, singing. Of course it was not such a performance as the great soloists at the New York opera house take a hand in, yet I am not sure but I receiv'd as much pleasure under the circumstances, sitting there, as I have had from the best Italian compositions, express'd by world-famous performers.... They sang very well, mostly quaint old songs and declamatory hymns, to fitting tunes. Here, for instance:

My days are swiftly gliding by, and I a pilgrim stranger,
Would not detain them as they fly, those hours of toil and danger;
For O we stand on Jordan's strand, our friends are passing over,
And just before, the shining shore we may almost discover.
We'll gird our loins my brethren dear, our distant home discerning,
Our absent Lord has left us word, let every lamp be burning,
For O we stand on Jordan's strand, our friends are passing over,
And just before, the shining shore we may almost discover.

105

August 12th, 1863—I see the President almost every day, as I happen to live where he passes to or from his lodgings out of town. He never sleeps at the White House during the hot season, but has quarters at a healthy location some three miles north of the city, the Soldiers' home, a United States military establishment. I saw him this morning about 8½ coming in to business, riding on Vermont avenue, near L street. He always has a company of twenty-five or thirty cavalry, with sabres drawn and held upright over their shoulders. They say this guard was against his personal wish, but he let his counselors have their way. The party makes no great show in uniform or horses. Mr. Lincoln on the saddle generally rides a good-sized, easy-going gray horse, is dress'd in plain black, somewhat rusty and dusty, wears a black stiff hat, and looks about as ordinary in attire, &c., as the commonest man. A Lieutenant, with yellow straps, rides at his left, and following behind, two by two, come the cavalry men, in their yellow-striped jackets. They are generally going at a slow trot, as

Walt Whitman, inscribed by him: "Taken from life 1863
war time Washington DC."

Lincoln, wrote Whitman, "has a face like a Hoosier Michael Angelo, so awful ugly it becomes beautiful, with its strange mouth, its deep cut, criss-cross lines, and its doughnut complexion."

Lincoln's photograph, annotated by Whitman

Wartime Washington, DC, with Trinity Church in the foreground, the new Capitol building going up in the distance, and, between them to the left, the white tops of hospital tents. Lincoln insisted, over the objections of some of his cabinet, that construction on the Capitol go forward during the war as a symbol of the Union's continuation.

A highly effective Secretary of War, appointed in 1862, Edwin M. Stanton was one of the most forceful Unionists in Lincoln's cabinet.

Charles Sumner, the prominent Republican senator from Mass-achusetts: one of the "big bugs" in Washington with whom Whitman spoke while trying to obtain a government job.

Ulysses S. Grant, the only consistently aggressive and mainly victorious commander of the Army of the Potomac, who in 1869 at his presidential inauguration asked for "patient forbearance one toward another throughout the land, and a determined effort on the part of every citizen to do his share toward cementing a happy union."

Robert E. Lee, whose clear-sighted desire during the postwar period to build up the South rather than brood over its defeat contributed appreciably to reconciling the South and the North.

The Washington headquarters of the United States Christian Commission, a private, voluntary organization to help soldiers, especially those who were sick and wounded.

The 110th Pennsylvania Infantry standing for inspection on April 24, 1863, eight days before the week-long battle of Chancellorsville.

Soldiers recovering in Campbell Hospital, Washington, from wounds received at Chancellorsville in early May 1863.

that is the pace set them by the one they wait upon. The sabres and accoutrements clank, and the entirely unornamental *cortège* as it trots towards Lafayette square arouses no sensation, only some curious stranger stops and gazes. I see very plainly ABRAHAM LINCOLN's dark brown face, with the deep-cut lines, the eyes, always to me with a deep latent sadness in the expression. We have got so that we exchange bows, and very cordial ones. Sometimes the President goes and comes in an open barouche. The cavalry always accompany him, with drawn sabres. Often I notice as he goes out evenings— and sometimes in the morning, when he returns early—he turns off and halts at the large and handsome residence of the Secretary of War, on K street, and holds conference there. If in his barouche, I can see from my window he does not alight, but sits in his vehicle, and Mr. Stanton comes out to attend him. Sometimes one of his sons, a boy of ten or twelve, accompanies him, riding at his right on a pony.

106

We are expecting to hear of more rows in New York about the draft; it commences there right away I see—this time it will be no such doings as a month or five weeks ago; the Gov't here is forwarding a large force of regulars to New York to be ready for anything that may happen—there will be no blank cartridges this time. Well, I thought when I first heard of the riot in N. Y. I had some feelings for them, but soon as I found what it really was, I felt it was the devil's own work all through. I guess the strong arm will be exhibited this time up to the shoulder.

107

...I saw in the New York papers (which get here about 5 every evening) the announcement of Charles Chauncey's death. When I went up to my room... towards 11 I took a seat by the open window in the splendid soft moonlit night, and, there alone by myself, (as is my custom sometimes under such circumstances), I devoted to the dead boy the silent cheerful tribute of an hour or so of floating thought about him, & whatever rose up from the thought of him, & his looks, his handsome face, his hilarious fresh ways, his sunny smile, his voice, his blonde hair, his talk, his caprices—the way he & I first met—how we spoke together impromptu, no introduction— then our easy falling into intimacy—he with his affectionate heart thought so well of me, & I loved him then, & love him now—I thought over our meetings together, our drinks & groups so friendly, our suppers with Fred & Charley Russell &c. off by ourselves at some table, at Pfaff's.... —O how charming those early times, adjusting our friendship, I to the three others, although it needed lit- tle adjustment—for I believe we all loved each other more than we supposed—Chauncey was frequently the life & soul of these gather- ings—was full of sparkle, & so good, really witty—then for an excep- tion he would have a mood come upon him & right after the onset of our party, he would grow still & cloudy & up & unaccountably depart—but these were seldom—then I got to having occasionally quite a long walk with him, only us two, & then he would talk well & freely about himself, his experiences, feelings, quite confidential, &c. All these I resumed, sitting by myself.

108

I was at the hospital yesterday as usual—I never miss a day. I go by my feelings—if I should feel that it would be better for me to lay by for a while, I should do so, but not while I feel so well as I do the past week, for all the hot weather; and while the chance lasts I would improve it, for by and by the night cometh when no man can work (ain't I getting pious!). I got a letter from Probasco yesterday; he sent $4 for my sick and wounded—

109

...for nearly two months and a half I have been in the habit of get- ting my own breakfast in my room and my dinner at a restaurant. I have a little spirit lamp, and always have a capital cup of tea, and some bread, and perhaps some preserved fruit; for dinner I get a

good plate of meat and plenty of potatoes, good and plenty for 25 or
30 cents. I hardly ever take any thing more than these two meals,
both of them are pretty hearty—

SEPTEMBER

110

—Here, now, is a specimen army hospital case: Lorenzo Strong, Co.
A, 9th United States Cavalry, shot by a shell last Sunday; right leg
amputated on the field. Sent up here Monday night, 14th. Seem'd to
be doing pretty well till Wednesday noon, 16th, when he took a turn
for the worse, and a strangely rapid and fatal termination ensued.
Though I had much to do, I staid and saw all. It was a death-picture
characteristic of these soldiers' hospitals—the perfect specimen of
physique, one of the most magnificent I ever saw—the convulsive
spasms and working of muscles, mouth, and throat. There are two
good women nurses, one on each side. The doctor comes in and gives
him a little chloroform. One of the nurses constantly fans him, for it
is fearfully hot. He asks to be rais'd up, and they put him in a half-
sitting posture. He call'd for "Mark" repeatedly, half-deliriously, all
day. Life ebbs, runs now with the speed of a mill race; his splendid
neck, as it lays all open, works still, slightly; his eyes turn back. A religious person coming in offers a prayer, in subdued tones, bent at the
foot of the bed; and in the space of the aisle, a crowd, including two
or three doctors, several students, and many soldiers, has silently
gather'd. It is very still and warm, as the struggle goes on, and dwin-
dles, a little more, and a little more—and then welcome oblivion,
painlessness, death. A pause, the crowd drops away, a white bandage
is bound around and under the jaw, the propping pillows are
removed, the limpsy head falls down, the arms are softly placed by
the side, all composed, all still,—and the broad white sheet is thrown
over everything.

111

—All around us here are forts, by the score—great ambulance &
teamsters' camps &c—these I go to—some have little hospitals, I
visit, &c &c—

112

You have no idea how many soldiers there are who have lost their
voices, and have to speak in whispers—there are a great many, I meet
some almost every day.

113

Ward F. bed 50, admitted Aug. 19, Co. B 111th Penn.—mother Mrs.
Melinda Morrison, Tidioute, Warren Co., Penn.—Fever, (only 15
yrs. old 22 Nov. '62)

　　Ward G, H, or I, young man I promised to come in to read to—
sick with fever—he cannot read steadily himself—his head swims—
take him the paper—

　　Ward D bed 37 Isaac Livenspargh, Co. H, 55th Ohio, gun shot
and left leg—admitted June 15th—father John Livenspargh, Lyken-
ston, Crawford Co., Ohio.

　　Ward K bed 37—Ashbury Allen—Co. D, 27th Indiana—diarrhea, bronchitis, & trouble in privates—some quince jelly—father
W. Allen, Noblesville, Hamilton Co. Ind.

　　Ward A. August 28-9—'63—Bethuel Smith—Co. F 2nd U.S.
Cavalry, wounded in foot, father Christopher Smith, Glen's Falls,
Warren Co., N.Y.

　　Ward H bed 3, Aug. 29 Willis Northrup, (age 19) Co. G. 108th
N.Y.—chronic pleuritis, pretty weak, has diarrhea—father Ranson
Northrup, Webster, Monroe Co., N.Y.—some brandy.

　　Ward A bed 41 Pleasant Borley—Co. A 1st Reg. Cavalry—gunshot wound left leg—brother John Borley, Epton P.O., Davis Co,
Ind.

114

...I have the consciousness of saving quite a number of lives by saving them from giving up—and being a good deal with them; the men say it is so, and the doctors say it is so—and I will candidly confess I can see it is true, though I say it of myself.

115

...my evenings are frequently spent in scenes that make a terrible difference—for I am still a hospital visitor, there has not passed a day for months (or at least not more than two) that I have not been among the sick & wounded, either in hospitals or down in camp— occasionally here I spend the evenings in hospital—the experience is a profound one, beyond all else, & touches me personally, egotistically, in unprecedented ways—I mean the way often the amputated, sick, sometimes dying soldiers cling & cleave to me as it were as a man overboard to a plank, & the perfect content they have if I will remain with them, sit on the side of the cot awhile, some youngsters often, & caress them &c.—It is delicious to be the object of so much love & reliance, & to do them such good, soothe & pacify torments of wounds &c—

116

—if I should pick out the most genuine Union men and real patriots I have ever met in all my experience, I should pick out two or three Tennessee and Virginia Unionists I have met in the hospitals, wounded or sick. One young man [is]... John Barker, 2nd Tennessee Vol. (Union), was a long while a prisoner in Secesh prisons in Georgia, and in Richmond—three times the devils hung him up by the heels to make him promise to give up his Unionism; once he was cut down for dead. He is a young married man with one child. His little property destroyed, his wife and child turned out—he hunted and tormented—and any moment he could have had anything if he would join the Confederacy—but he was firm as a rock; he would not even take an oath to not fight for either side.... He is a large, slow, good-natured man, somehow made me often think of father; shrewd, very little to say—wouldn't talk to anybody but me. His whole thought was to get back and fight; he was not fit to go, but he has gone back to Tennessee.

117

Among other sights [about Washington] are immense droves of cattle with their drivers, passing through the streets of the city.

118

...fancy to yourself a space of three to twenty acres of ground, on which are group'd ten or twelve very large wooden barracks, with, perhaps, a dozen or twenty, and sometimes more than that number, small buildings, capable altogether of accommodating from five hundred to a thousand or fifteen hundred persons.... Within sight of the capitol, as I write, are some thirty or forty such collections, at times holding from fifty to seventy thousand men.... Through the rich August verdure of the trees, see that white group of buildings off yonder in the outskirts; then another cluster half a mile to the left of the first; then another a mile to the right, and another a mile beyond, and still another between us and the first. Indeed, we can hardly look in any direction but these clusters are dotting the landscape and environs. That little town, as you might suppose it, off there on the brow of a hill, is indeed a town, but of wounds, sickness, and death. It is Finley hospital, northeast of the city, on Kendall green, as it used to be call'd. That other is Campbell hospital. Both are large establishments. I have known these two alone to have from two thousand to twenty five hundred inmates.

119

...I am in the hospitals as usual—I stand it better the last three weeks than ever before—I go among the worst fevers and wounds with impunity. I go among the smallpox, etc., just the same—I feel to go without apprehension, and so I go.

...one's heart grows sick of war, after all, when you see what it really is; every once in a while I feel so horrified and disgusted—it seems to me like a great slaughter-house and the men mutually butchering each other—then I feel how impossible it appears, again, to retire from this contest, until we have carried our points (it is cruel to be so tossed from pillar to post in one's judgment). Washington is a pleasant place in some respects—it has the finest trees, and plenty of them everywhere, on the streets and grounds. The Capitol grounds, though small, have the finest cultivated trees I ever see—there is a great variety, and not one but is in perfect condition.... The great sights of Washington are the public buildings, the wide streets, the public grounds, the trees, the Smithsonian institute and grounds. I go to the latter occasionally—the institute is an old fogy concern, but the grounds are fine. Sometimes I go up to Georgetown, about two and a half miles up the Potomac, an old town—just opposite it in the river is an island, where the niggers have their first Washington reg't encamped. They make a good show, are often seen in the streets of Washington in squads. Since they have begun to carry arms, the Secesh here in Georgetown (about three fifths) are not insulting to them as formerly.

Scene in the woods on the Peninsula—told me by Milton Roberts, Ward G (Maine)—After the battle of White Oaks Church on the retreat, the march at night—the scene between 12 & 2 o'clock that night at the church in the woods, the hospital show at night, the wounded brought in—previous the silent stealthy march through the woods, at times stumbling on the bodies of dead men in the road, (there had been terrible fights there that day, only closing at dark)— we retreating, the artillery horses feet muffled, orders that men should tread light & only speak in whispers—

Then between midnight & 2 o'clock we halted to rest a couple of hours at an opening in the woods—in this opening was a pretty good sized old church used impromptu for a hospital for the wounded of the battles of the day thereabout—with these it was filled, all varieties horrible beyond description—the darkness dimly lit with candles, lamps, torches moving about, but plenty of darkness & half darkness—the crowds of wounded bloody & pale, the surgeons operating—the yards outside also filled—they lay on the ground, some on blankets, some on stray planks,—the despairing screams & curses of some out of their senses, the murky darkness, the gleaming of the torches, the smoke from them too, the doctors operating, the scent of chloroform, the glistening of the steel instruments as the flash of lamps falls upon them.

—at Antietam there was a very large barn & farm house—the barn was filled with wounded, & the barn yard, and the house as full as it could stick—a peaceful barn, now bloody, the fragrant hay they used to place the men on for operations—they turned the cattle out of their stalls.

122

...get my breakfast in my room in the morning myself, and dinner at a restaurant about 3 o'clock—I get along very well and very economical....

123

...two wounded officers come in to get their pay—one has crutches; the other is drest in the light-blue uniform of the invalid corps. Way up here on the 5th floor it is pretty hard scratching for cripples and very weak men to journey up here—often they come up here very weary and faint, and then find out they can't get their money, some red-tape hitch, and the poor soldiers look so disappointed—it always makes me feel bad.

124

Sometimes I see women in the hospitals, mothers come to see their sons, and occasionally one that makes me think of my dear mother—one did very much, a lady about 60, from Pennsylvania, come to see her son, a captain....

125

There is a new lot of wounded now again. They have been arriving sick and wounded for three days—first long strings of ambulances with the sick, but yesterday many with bad and bloody wounds, poor fellows. I thought I was cooler and more used to it, but the sight of some of them brought tears into my eyes.... I had the good luck yesterday to do quite a good deal of good. I had provided a lot of nourishing things for the men, but for another quarter—but I had them where I could use them immediately for these new wounded as they came in faint and hungry, and fagged out with a long rough journey, all dirty and torn, and many pale as ashes and all bloody. I distributed all my stores, gave partly to the nurses I knew that were just taking charge of them—and as many as I could fed myself. Then besides I found a lot of oyster soup handy, and I procured it all at once.... It is the most pitiful sight, I think, when first the men are brought in. I have to bustle round, to keep from crying—they are such rugged young men—all these just arrived are cavalry men. Our troops got the worst of it, but fought like devils. Our men engaged were Kilpatrick's Cavalry. They were in the rear as part of Meade's retreat, and the Reb cavalry cut in between and cut them off and attacked them and shelled them terribly.

126

One realizes here in Washington the great labors, even the negative ones, of Lincoln; that it is a big thing to have just kept the United States from being thrown down and having its throat cut. I have not waver'd or had any doubt of the issue, since Gettysburg.

127

We are soon to see a thing accomplished here which I have often exercised my mind about, namely, the putting of the Genius of America away up there on the top of the dome of the Capitol.

Of our Genius of America, a sort of compound of handsome Choctaw squaw with the well-known Liberty of Rome, (and the French revolution,) and a touch perhaps of Athenian Pallas, (but very faint,) it is to be further described as an extensive female, cast in bronze, with much drapery, especially ruffles. The Genius has for a year or two past been standing in the mud, west of the Capitol; I saw her there all Winter, looking very harmless and innocent, although holding a huge sword. For pictorial representation of the Genius, see any five-dollar United States greenback; for there she is at the left hand. But the artist has made her twenty times brighter in expression, &c., than the bronze Genius is.

I have curiosity to know the effect of this figure crowning the dome. The pieces, as I have said, are at present all separated, ready to be hoisted to their place. On the Capitol generally, much work remains to be done.... I have grown so used to the sight, over the Capitol, of a certain huge derrick which has long surmounted the dome, swinging its huge one-arm now south, now north, &c., that I believe I shall have a sneaking sorrow when they remove it and substitute the Genius. (I would not dare to say that there is something about this powerful, simple and obedient piece of machinery, so modern, so significant in many respects of our constructive nation and age, and even so poetical, that I have even balanced in my mind, how it would do to leave the rude and mighty derrick atop o' the Capitol there, as fitter emblem, may be, than Choctaw girl and Pallas.)

128

...it is lucky I like Washington in many respects, and that things are upon the whole pleasant personally, for every day of my life I see enough to make one's heart ache with sympathy and anguish here in the hospitals, and I do not know as I could stand it if it was not counterbalanced outside. It is curious, when I am present at the most appalling things—deaths, operations, sickening wounds (perhaps full of maggots)—I do not fail, although my sympathies are very much excited, but keep singularly cool; but often hours afterward, perhaps when I am home or out walking alone, I feel sick and actually tremble when I recall the thing and have it in my mind again before me.

129

...at 14th and L street a stout young woman wheeling a wheelbarrow—the wench perhaps 15 years old, black and jolly and strong as a horse;—in the wheelbarrow, cuddled up, a child-wench, of six or seven years, equally black, shining black, and jolly with an old quilt around here, sitting plump back, riding backwards, partially holding on, a little fearful, and trying to hold in her arms a full grown lap-dog—the child-wench bareheaded; and all, the dog, the stout-armed negress, firmly holding the handles, and pushing on through the mud—the heads of the pretty silver dog, and of the pictorial black, round and young, with alert eyes as she turned half way around, twisting her neck anxious to see what prospect, (having probably been overturned in the mud on some previous occasion)—the gait of the big girl, so sturdy and so graceful with her short petticoats—her legs stepping, pushing steadily along through obstructions—the shining curl'd dog, standing up in the hold of the little one,—she huddled in the barrow, riding backwards, with the patch-work quilt around her, sitting down, her feet visible poking straight out in front—made a passing group which as I stopt to look at it, you may if you choose stop and imagine.

130

...there are always special cases calling for something special.... Poor fellows, how young they are, lying there with their pale faces, and that mute look in their eyes.

131

...[the ambulances] are always going. Sometimes from the river, coming up through Seventh street, you can see a long, long string of them, slowing wending, each vehicle filled with sick or wounded soldiers, just brought up from the front from the region once down toward Falmouth, now out toward Warrenton. Again, from a boat that has just arrived, a load of our paroled men from the Southern prisons, *via* Fortress Monroe. Many of these will be fearfully sick and ghastly from their treatment at Richmond, &c. Hundreds, though originally young and strong men, never recuperate again from their experience in these Southern prisons.... You mark the forms huddled on the bottom of these wagons; you mark yellow and emaciated faces. Some are supporting others. I constantly see instances of tenderness in this way from the wounded to those worse wounded.

132

—As I write I sit in a large pretty well-fill'd ward by the cot of a lad of 18 belonging to Company M, 2d N Y cavalry, wounded three weeks ago to-day at Culpepper—hit by fragment of a shell in the leg below the knee—a large part of the calf of the leg is torn away, (it killed his horse)—still no bones broken, but a pretty large ugly wound—I have been writing to his mother at Comac, Suffolk co. N Y—She must have a letter just as if from him, about every three days—it pleases the boy very much—has four sisters—them also I have to write to occasionally—Although so young he has been in many fights & tells me shrewdly about them, but only when I ask him—He is a cheerful good-natured child—has to lie in bed constantly, his leg in a box—I bring him things—he says little or nothing in the way of thanks—is a country boy—always smiles & brightens much when I appear—looks straight in my face & never at what I may have in my hand for him—

133

...I think I have an instinct & faculty for these cases. Poor young men, how many have I seen, & known—how pitiful it is to see them—one must be calm & cheerful, & not let on how their case really is, must stop much with them, find their idiosyncrasies—do any thing for them—nourish them, judiciously give the right things to drink—bring in the affections, soothe them, brace them up, kiss them, discard all ceremony, & fight for them, as it were, with all weapons.... Such work blesses him that works as much as the object of it. I have never been happier than in some of these hospital ministering hours.

134

—I provide myself with a lot of bright new 10ct & 5ct bills, & when I give little sums of change I give the bright new bills. Every little thing even must be taken advantage of—to give bright fresh 10ct bills, instead of any other, helps break the dullness of hospital life—

135

There are some 25 or 30 wards, barracks, tents, &c in [Armory Square] hospital— ...ward C has beds for 60 patients, they are mostly full—most of the other principal wards about the same— so you see a U S general hospital here is quite an establishment—this has a regular police, armed sentries at the gates & in the passages &c.—& a great staff of surgeons, cadets, women & men nurses &c &c. I come here pretty regularly because this hospital receives I think the worst cases & is one of the least visited—there is not much hospital visiting here now—it has become an old story—the principal here, Dr Bliss, is a very fine operating surgeon—sometimes he performs several amputations or other operations of importance in a day—amputations, blood, death are nothing here—

136

It is quite an art to visit the hospitals to advantage.

137

I have moved to a new room, 456 Sixth street, not far from Pennsylvania avenue... & not far from the Capitol–it is in 3d story, an addition back, seems to be going to prove a very good winter room, as it is right under the roof & looks south, has low windows, is plenty big

enough, I have gas—I think the lady will prove a good woman… —
one thing is I am quite by myself, there is no passage up there except
to my room, & right off against my side of the house is a great old
yard with grass & some trees back, & the sun shines in all day &c. &
it smells sweet & good air, good big bed, I sleep first rate—

138

I am excellent well. I have cut my beard short, & hair ditto: (all my
acquaintances are in anger & despair & go about wringing their
hands). My face is all tanned & red. If the weather is moist or has
been lately, or looks as if it thought of going to be, I perambulate this
land in big army boots outside & up to my knees. Then around my
majestic brow, around my well-brimmed felt hat—a black & gold
cord with acorns. Altogether the effect is satisfactory. The guards as
I enter or pass places often salute me.

139

[from a letter to Louisa van Velsor Whitman]

Mother, if any of my soldier boys should ever call upon you (as they
are often anxious to have my address in Brooklyn) you just use them
as you know how to without ceremony, and if you happen to have pot
luck and feel to ask them to take a bite, don't be afraid to do so. There
is one very good boy, Thos. Neat, 2nd N. Y. Cavalry, wounded in leg.
He is now home on furlough—his folks live, I think, in Jamaica. He
is a noble boy. He may call upon you. (I gave him here $1 toward buy-
ing his crutches, &c.) I like him very much. Then possibly a Mr.
Haskell, or some of his folks from Western New York, may call—he
had a son died here, a very fine boy. I was with him a good deal, and
the old man and his wife have written me, and asked me my address
in Brooklyn. He said he had children in N. Y. city and was occasionally down there. Mother, when I come home I will show you
some of the letters I get from mothers, sisters, fathers, &c.—they will
make you cry.

140

—To-night, after leaving the hospital at 10 o'clock, (I had been on self-imposed duty some five hours, pretty closely confined,) I wander'd a long time around Washington. The night was sweet, very clear, sufficiently cool, a voluptuous half-moon, slightly golden, the space near it of a transparent blue-gray tinge. I walk'd up Pennsylvania avenue, and then to Seventh street, and a long while around the Patent-office. Somehow it look'd rebukefully strong, majestic, there in the delicate moonlight. The sky, the planets, the constellations all so bright, so calm, so expressively silent, so soothing, after those hospital scenes. I wander'd to and fro till the moist moon set, long after midnight.

141

—to think it will soon be a year I have been away! It has passed away very swiftly, somehow, to me. O what things I have witnessed during that time—I shall never forget them. And the war is not settled yet, and one does not see anything at all certain about the settlement yet; but I have finally got for good, I think, into the feeling that our triumph is assured, whether it be sooner or whether it be later, or whatever roundabout way we are led there, and I find I don't change that conviction from any reverses we meet, or any delays or Government blunders. There are blunders enough, heaven knows, but I am thankful things have gone on as well for us as they have—thankful the ship rides safe and sound at all. Then I have finally made up my mind that Mr. Lincoln has done as good as a human man could do.

142

…how passing deep and tender these boys [are]. Some have died, but the love for them lives as long as I draw breath. These soldiers know how to love too, when once they have the right person and the right love offered them. It is wonderful.… I am writing this note this afternoon in Major H's office—he is away sick—I am here a good deal of the time alone. It is a dark rainy afternoon—we don't know what is going on down in front, whether Meade is getting the worst of it or not—

NOVEMBER

143

Well, poor John Mahay is dead. He died yesterday. His was a painful and long-lingering case.... He belonged to company A, 101st New York, and was shot through the lower region of the abdomen at second Bull Run, August, '62. One scene at his bedside will suffice for the agonies of nearly two years. The bladder had been perforated by a bullet going entirely through him. Not long since I sat a good part of the morning by his bedside, ward E, Armory square. The water ran out of his eyes from the intense pain, and the muscles of his face were distorted, but he utter'd nothing except a low groan now and then. Hot moist cloths were applied, and reliev'd him somewhat. Poor Mahay, a mere boy in age, but old in misfortune. He never knew the love of parents, was placed in infancy in one of the New York charitable institutions, and subsequently bound out to a tyrannical master in Sullivan county, (the scars of whose cowhide and club remain'd yet on his back.) His wound here was a most disagreeable one, for he was a gentle, cleanly, and affectionate boy. He found friends in his hospital life, and, indeed, was a universal favorite. He had quite a funeral ceremony.

144

—I am now home at my mother's in Brooklyn N Y—I am in good health as ever & eat my rations without missing one time— ...I came through from Washington to New York by day train, 2d Nov., had a very pleasant trip, every thing went lovely, & I got home in the evening between 8 and 9—Next morning I went up to the polls bright & early— ...we have gained a great victory in this city—it went union this time, though it went democratic strong only a year ago, & for many years past—& all through the state the election was a very big thing for the union—I tell you the copperheads got flaxed out handsomely—indeed these late elections are about as great a victory for us as if we had flaxed General Lee himself, & all his men....

Two or three nights ago I went to the N Y Academy of Music, to the Italian opera.... It is in a splendid great house, four or five tiers high, & a broad parquette on the main floor. The opera here now has some of the greatest singers in the world—the principal lady singer (her name is Medori) has a voice that would make you hold your breath with wonder & delight, it is like a miracle—no mocking bird nor the clearest flute can begin with it—besides it is [a] very rich & strong voice—& besides she is a tall & handsome lady, & her actions are so graceful as she moves about the stage, playing her part.... [In] one scene in the opera I saw—things have worked so in the piece that this lady is compelled, although she tries very hard to avoid it, to give a cup of poisoned wine to her lover—the king her husband forces her to do it—she pleads hard, but her husband threatens to take both their lives (all this is in singing & music, very fine)—so the lover is brought in as a prisoner, & the king pretends to pardon him & make up, & asks the young man to drink a cup of wine, & orders the lady to pour it out. The lover drinks it, then the king gives her & him a look, & smiles & walks off the stage. And now came as good a piece of performance as I ever saw in my life. The lady as soon as she saw that her husband was really gone, she sprang to her lover, clutched him by the arm, & poured out the greatest singing you ever heard—it poured like a raging river more than any thing else I could compare it to—she tells him he is poisoned—he tries to inquire &c and hardly knows what to make of it—she breaks in, trying to pacify him, & explain &c—all this goes on very rapid indeed, & the band accompanying—she quickly draws out from her bosom a little vial, to neutralize the poison, then the young man in his desperation abuses her & tells her perhaps it is to poison him still more as she has already poisoned him once—this puts her in such agony, she begs & pleads with him to take the antidote at once before it is too late—her voice is so wild & high it goes through one like a knife, yet it is delicious—she holds the little vial to his mouth with one hand & with the other springs open a secret door in the wall, for him to escape from the palace—he swallows the antidote, & as she pushes him through he door, the husband returns with some armed guards, but she slams the door to, & stands back up against the door, & her arms spread wide open across it, one fist clenched, & her eyes glaring like a wild cat, so they dare not touch her—& that ends the scene... all this is in singing & music, & lots of it too, on a big scale, in the band, every instrument you can think of, & the best players in the world, & sometimes the whole band & the whole men's chorus & women's chorus all putting on the steam together—& all in a vast house, light as day, & with a crowded audience of ladies & men. Such singing & strong rich music always give me the greatest pleasure—& so the opera is the only amusement I have gone to, for my own satisfaction, for [the] last ten years.

145

...it looks so different here in all this mighty city, every thing going with a big rush & so gay, as if there was neither war nor hospitals in the land. New York & Brooklyn appear nothing but prosperity & plenty. Every where carts & trucks & carriages & vehicles on the go, loaded with goods, express-wagons, omnibuses, cars, &c—thousands of ships along the wharves, & the piers piled high, where they are loading or unloading the cargoes—all the stores crammed with every thing you can think of, & the markets with all sorts of provisions—tens & hundreds of thousands of people every where, (the population is 1,500,000), almost every body well-drest, & appearing to have enough—then the splendid river & harbor here, full of ships, steamers, sloops, &c—then the great street, Broadway, for four miles, one continual jam of people, & the great magnificent stores all along on each side, & the show windows filled with beautiful & costly goods—I never saw the crowd thicker, nor such goings on & such prosperity—& as I passed through Baltimore & Philadelphia it seemed to be just the same.

146

—I have now been home about a week in the midst of relations, &
many friends, many young men, some I have known from childhood,
many I love very much. I am out quite a good deal, as we are glad to
be with each other—they have entertainments &c.... My friends
among the young men make supper parties, after which there is
drinking &c., every thing prodigal & first rate, one, Saturday night,
& another last night—it is much pleasure, yet often in the midst of
the profusion, the palatable dishes to eat, & the laughing & talking,
& liquors &c, my thoughts silently turn to Washington, to all who
lie there sick & wounded, with bread & molasses for supper—

147

My New York boys are good, too good—if I staid here a month
longer I should be killed with kindness—The great recompense of
my journey here is to see my mother so well, & so bravely sailing on
amid many troubles & discouragements like a noble old ship—My
brother Andrew is bound for another world—he is here the greater
part of the time—

   ...I think sometimes to be a woman is greater than to be a
man—is more eligible to greatness, not the ostensible article, but the
real one.

148

...I hope it will be so ordered to let things go as easy as possible with
all my dear boys wounded or sick, & I hope it will be God's will that
we shall all meet again, my dear loving comrades, not only here but
hereafter.

149

I feel to devote myself more to the work of my life, which is making
poems. I must bring out Drum Taps. I *must* be continually bringing
out poems—now is the hey day. I shall range along the high plateau
of my life & capacity for a few years now, & then swiftly descend.

The life here in the cities, & the objects, &c of most, seem to me very flippant & shallow somehow since I returned this time—

DECEMBER

150

...how young & how American [the soldiers] mostly are—so on my own account I shall continue as a Missionary among them as surely as I live—& shall continue for years.... I reject none of course—not rebel wounded nor blacks nor any when I find them suffering and dying.

Second Year of Service, 1864

Address delivered at the dedication of the Cemetery at Gettysburg.

Four score and seven years ago our fathers brought forth on this continent, a new nation, conceived in Liberty, and dedicated to the proposition that all men are created equal.

Now we are engaged in a great civil war, testing whether that nation, or any nation so conceived and so dedicated, can long endure. We are met on a great battle-field of that war. We have come to dedicate a portion of that field, as a final resting place for those who here gave their lives, that that nation might live. It is altogether fitting and proper that we should do this.

But, in a larger sense, we can not dedicate — we can not consecrate — we can not hallow — this ground. The brave men, living and dead, who struggled here, have consecrated it, far above our poor power to add or detract. The world will little note, nor long remember what we say here, but it can

A page from the final draft of the Gettysburg Address in Lincoln's hand, dated November 19, 1863.

JANUARY

151

CONGRESS WILL PROBABLY KEEP in session till well into the summer. As to what course things will take, political or military, there's no telling. I think, though, the Secesh military power is getting more and more shaky. How they can make any headway against our new, large, and fresh armies next season passes my wit to see.

152

In the present struggle, as already seen and review'd, probably three-fourths of the losses, men, lives, &c., have been sheer superfluity, extravagance, waste.

153

—After the battles at Columbia, Tennessee, where we repuls'd about a score of vehement rebel charges, they left a great many wounded on the ground, mostly within our range. Whenever any of these wounded attempted to move away by any means, generally by crawling off, our men without exception brought them down by a bullet. They let none crawl away, no matter what his condition.

154

In one of the late movements of our troops in the valley, (near Upperville, I think,) a strong force of Moseby's mounted guerillas attack'd a train of wounded, and the guard of cavalry convoying them. The ambulances contained about 60 wounded, quite a number of them officers of rank. The rebels were in strength , and the capture of the train and its partial guard after a short snap was effectually accomplish'd. No sooner had our men surrender'd, the rebels instantly commenced robbing the train and murdering their prisoners, even the wounded. Here is the scene of a sample of it, ten minutes after. Among the wounded officers in the ambulances were one, a lieutenant of regulars, and another of higher rank. These two were-dragg'd out on the ground on their backs, and were now surrounded by the guerillas, a demoniac crowd, each member of which was stabbing them in different parts of their bodies. One of the officers had his feet pinn'd firmly to the ground by bayonets stuck through them and thrust into the ground. These two officers, as afterwards found on examination, had receiv'd about twenty such thrusts, some of them through the mouth, face, &c. The wounded had all been dragg'd (to give a better chance also for plunder,) out of their wagons; some had been effectually dispatch'd, and their bodies were lying there lifeless and bloody. Others, not yet dead, but horribly mutilated, were moaning or groaning. Of our men who surrender'd, most had been thus maim'd or slaughter'd.

At this instant a force of our cavalry, who had been following the train at some interval, charged suddenly upon the secesh captors, who proceeded at once to make the best escape they could. Most of them got away, but we gobbled two officers and seventeen men, in the very acts just described. The sight was one which admitted of little discussion, as may be imagined. The seventeen capture'd men and two officers were put under guard for the night, but it was decided there and then that they should die. The next morning the two officers were taken in the town, separate places, put in the centre of the street, and shot. The seventeen men were taken to an open ground, a little one side. They were placed in a hollow square, half-encompass'd by two of our cavalry regiments, one of which regiments had three days before found the bloody corpses of three of their men hamstrung and hung up by the heels to limbs of trees by Moseby's guerillas, and the other had not long before had twelve men, after surrendering, shot and then hung by the neck to limbs of trees, and jeering inscriptions pinn'd to the breast of one of the corpses, who had been a sergeant. Those three, and those twelve, had been found, I say, by these environing regiments. Now, with revolvers, they for-m'd the grim cordon of the seventeen prisoners. The latter were placed in the midst of the hollow square, unfasten'd, and the ironical remark made to them that they were now to be given "a chance for themselves." A few ran for it. But what use? From every side the deadly pills came. In a few minutes the seventeen corpses strew'd the hollow square. I was curious to know whether some of the Union soldiers, some few, (some one or two at least of the youngsters,) did not abstain from shooting on the helpless men. Not one. There was no exultation, very little said, almost nothing, yet every man there contributed his shot.

FEBRUARY

155

There has been several hundred sick soldiers brought in here yester-day. I have been around among them to-day all day—it is enough to make me heart-sick, the old times over again; they are many of them mere wrecks, though young men (sickness is worse in some respects than wounds). One boy about 16, from Portland, Maine, only came from home a month ago, a recruit; he is here now very sick and down-hearted, poor child. He is a real country boy; I think has con-sumption. He was only a week with his reg't. I sat with him a long time; I saw [it] did him great good. I have been feeding some their dinners. It makes me feel quite proud, I find so frequently I can do with the men what no one else at all can, getting them to eat (some that will not touch their food otherwise, nor for anybody else)—it is sometimes quite affecting.... I found such a case to-day, a soldier with throat disease, very bad. I fed him quite a dinner; the men, his comrades around, just stared in wonder, and one of them told me afterwards that he (the sick man) had not eat so much at a meal in three months.

Culpepper, [Virginia,] where I am stopping, looks like a place of two or three thousand inhabitants. Must be one of the pleasantest towns in Virginia. Even now, dilapidated fences, all broken down, windows out, it has the remains of much beauty. I am standing on an eminence overlooking the town, though within its limits. To the west the long Blue Mountain range is very plain, looks quite near, though from 30 to 50 miles distant, with some gray splashes of snow yet visible. The show is varied and fascinating. I see a great eagle up there in the air sailing with pois'd wings, quite low. Squads of red legged soldiers are drilling; I suppose some of the new men of the Brooklyn 14th; they march off presently with muskets on their shoulders. In another place, just below me, are some soldiers squaring off logs to build a shanty—chopping away, and the noise of the axes sounding sharp. I hear the bellowing, unmusical screech of the mule. I mark the thin blue smoke rising from camp fires. Just below me is a collection of hospital tents, with a yellow flag elevated on a stick, and moving languidly in the breeze. Two discharged men (I know them both) are just leaving. One is so weak he can hardly walk; the other is stronger, and carries his comrade's musket. They move slowly along the muddy road toward the depot. The scenery is full of breadth, and spread on the most generous scale (everywhere in Virginia this thought fill'd me).... There is every day the sound of the wood-chopping axe, and the plentiful sight of negroes, crows, and mud. I note large droves and pens of cattle. The teamsters have camps of their own, and I go often among them. The officers occasionally invite me to dinner or supper at headquarters. The fare is plain, but you get something good to drink, and plenty of it. Gen. Meade is absent; Sedgwick is in command.

157

—I am down here pretty well toward the extreme front of the Army, eight or ten miles south of headquarters, (Brandy Station)—We had some fighting here, below here on picket lines, day before yesterday—We feared they, the rebs, were advancing upon us in our depleted condition, especially feared their making a flank movement up on our right. We were all ready to skedaddle from here last night, & expected it—horses harnessed in all directions, & traps packed up, (we have held & lost Culpepper three or four times already)—but I was very sleepy & laid down & went to sleep, never slept fresher or sweeter—but orders came during the night to stay for the present, there was no danger—during the night I heard tremendous yells, I got up & went out, & found it was some of the men returning from the extreme front—As day before yesterday a strong force, three corps, were moved down there—These were portions of them now returning—it was a curious sight to see the shadowy columns coming in two or three o'clock at night—I talked with the men—how good, how cheerful, how full of manliness & good nature our American young men are—I staid last night at the house of a real secesh woman, Mrs. Ashby—her husband (dead) a near relation of the famous reb Gen Ashby—she gave me a good supper & bed—

158

Dilapidated, fenceless, and trodden with war as Virginia is, wherever I move across her surface, I find myself rous'd to surprise and admiration. What capacity for products, improvements, human life, nourishment and expansion. Everywhere that I have been in the Old Dominion, (the subtle mockery of that title now!) such thoughts have fill'd me. The soil is yet far above the average of any of the northern States. And how full of breadth the scenery, everywhere distant mountains, everywhere convenient rivers. Even yet prodigal in forest woods, and surely eligible for all the fruits, orchards, and flowers. The skies and atmosphere most luscious, as I feel certain, from more than a year's residence in the State, and movements hither and yon. I should say very healthy, as a general thing. Then a rich and elastic quality, by night and by day. The sun rejoices in his strength, dazzling and burning, and yet, to me, never unpleasantly weakening. It is not the panting tropical heat, but invigorates. The north tempers it. The nights are often unsurpassable. Last evening (Feb. 8,) I saw the first of the new moon, the outlined old moon clear along with it; the sky and air so clear, such transparent hues of color, it seem'd to me I had never really seen the new moon before. It was the thinnest cut crescent possible. It hung delicate just above the sulky shadow of the Blue mountains. Ah, if it might prove an omen and good prophecy for this unhappy State.

159

The famous Brooklyn 14th are here, guarding the town. You see their red legs actively moving every where. Then they have a theatre of their own here. They give musical performances, nearly everything done capitally. Of course the audience is a jam. It is good sport to attend one of these entertainments of the 14th. I like to look around at the soldiers, and the general collection in front of the curtain, more than the scene on the stage.

160

Culpepper, Va.
Feb. 12, 1864

...I have no difficulty at all in making myself at home among the soldiers, teamsters, or any—I most always find they like to have me very much; it seems to do them good. No doubt they soon feel that my heart and sympathies are truly with them, and it is both a novelty and pleases them and touches their feelings, and so doubtless does them good—and I am sure it does that to me. There is more fun around here than you would think for.

161

Culpepper

Three or four days ago General S., who is now in chief command, (I believe Meade is absent, sick,) moved a strong force southward from camp as if intending business. They went to the Rapidan; there has since been some manoeuvring and little fighting, but nothing of consequence. The telegraphic accounts given Monday morning last, make entirely too much of it, I should say. What General S. intended we here know not, but we trust in that competent commander.

Culpepper, Va.

I have been in the division hospitals around here. There are not many men sick here, and no wounded—they now send them on to Washington. I shall return there in a few days, as I am very clear that the real need of one's services is there after all—there the worst cases concentrate, and probably will, while the war lasts.... What we call hospital here in the field is nothing but a collection of tents on the bare ground for a floor—rather hard accommodation for a sick man. They heat them there by digging a long trough in the ground under them, covering it over with old railroad iron and earth, and then building a fire at one end and letting it draw through and go out at the other, as both ends are open. This heats the ground through the middle of the hospital quite hot. I find some poor creatures crawling about pretty weak with diarrhoea; there is a great deal of that; they keep them until they get very bad indeed, and then send them to Washington. This aggravates the complaint, and they come into Washington in a terrible condition.... How often and how many have I seen come into Washington from this awful complaint after such an experience as I have described—with the look of death on their poor young faces; they keep them so long in the field hospitals with poor accommodations the disease gets too deeply seated.

To-day I have been out among some of the camps of the 2nd division of the 1st Corps. I have been wandering around all day, and have had a very good time, over woods, hills, and gullies—indeed, a real soldier's march. The weather is good and the travelling quite tolerable. I have been in the camps of some Massachusetts, Pennsylvania, and New York regiments. I have friends in them, and went out to see them, and see soldiering generally, as I can never cease to crave more and more knowledge of actual soldiers' life, and to be among them as much as possible.

One of the things to note here now is the arrival of the paymaster with his strong box, and the payment of bounties to veterans re-enlisting. Major H. is here to-day, with a small mountain of green-backs, rejoicing the hearts of the 2d division of the First corps. In the midst of a rickety shanty, behind a little table, sit the major and clerk Eldridge, with the rolls before them, and much moneys. A re-enlisted man gets in cash about $200 down, (and heavy instalments following, as the pay-days arrive, one after another.) The show of the men crowding around is quite exhilarating; I like to stand and look. They feel elated, their pockets full, and the ensuing furlough, the visit home. It is a scene of sparkling eyes and flush'd cheeks. The soldier has many gloomy and harsh experiences, and this makes up for some of them. Major H. is order'd to pay first all the re-enlisted men of the First corps their bounties and back pay, and then the rest. You hear the peculiar sound of the rustling of the new and crisp green-backs by the hour, through the nimble fingers of the major and my friend clerk E.

165

The troops here are scattered all around, much more apart than they seemed to me to be opposite Fredericksburg last winter. They mostly have good huts and fireplaces, etc. I have been to a great many of the camps, and I must say I am astonished [how] good the houses are almost everywhere. I have not seen one regiment, nor any part of one, in the poor uncomfortable little shelter tents that I saw so common last winter after Fredericksburg—but all the men have built huts of logs and mud.

166

[Washington]

For the past few weeks I have been on a tour down to the front, through the division hospitals especially those around Culpepper & Brandy Station, mostly of the 1st, 2d, & 3d corps to see how the sick were situated there.... I was much in contact with the rank in file, lived among them in their camps, among the common soldiers & teamsters, &c. I never go among the Army in this way, but what, after making all allowances, I feel that our general stock of young men shows all other races, meagre & pale & puny in comparison. The more I see of them in the army, the higher & broader my estimate of them.

167

I am back again... on my regular daily and nightly rounds.

MARCH

168

—Saw a large squad of our own deserters, (over 300) surrounded with a cordon of arm'd guards, marching along Pennsylvania avenue. The most motley collection I ever saw, all sorts of rig, all sorts of hats and caps, many fine-looking young fellows, some of them shame-faced, some sickly, most of them dirty, shirts very dirty and long worn, &c. They tramp'd along without order, a huge huddling mass, not in ranks. I saw some of the spectators laughing, but I felt like anything else but laughing. These deserters are far more numerous than would be thought. Almost every day I see squads of them, sometimes two or three at a time, with a small guard; sometimes ten or twelve, under a larger one. (I hear that desertions from the army now in the field have often averaged 10,000 a month. One of the commonest sights in Washington is a squad of deserters.)

169

I had an idea before I left Brooklyn that our army had at least a large proportion of foreign born soldiers. What it has of that kind seems to me to amount to little or nothing.

170

We have had quite a snow storm, but [it] is clear and sunny to-day here, but sloshy. I am wearing my army boots—anything but the dust.... If I can get a chance I think I shall [go] home for a while. I want to try to bring out a book of poems, a new one, to be called "Drum-Taps," and I want to come to New York for that purpose, too.

171

...the sick are coming in here now from [the] front pretty freely. I have need of means additional—The new sick & wounded generally come in without a cent. I give aid of all kinds, sometimes little sums of money.... [I would like to have] some 20 or $25 the ensuing week, if possible, for it is for a sacred object.

172

...I think it worse than ever here in the hospitals. We are getting the dregs as it were of the sickness and awful hardships of the past three years. There is the most horrible cases of diarrhoea you ever conceived of, and by the hundreds of thousands; I suppose from such diet as they have in the army.... Every one is so unfeeling; it has got to be an old story. There is no good nursing.... I feel so sick when I see what kind of people there are among them, with charge over them—so cold and ceremonious, afraid to touch them.

173

It is dusty and chilly to-day, anything but agreeable. Gen. Grant is expected every moment now in the Army of the Potomac to take active command. I have just this moment heard from the front—there is nothing yet of a movement, but each side is continually on the alert, expecting something to happen.

*Walt Whitman in the second year of his service
as a self-designated "Army Hospital Visitor."*

Union soldier dismembered by a cannon ball during the
battle at Gettysburg, Pennsylvania, July 1863.

Confederate soldier killed in the defense of Petersburg,
Virginia, April 1865, the final month of the war.

(ABOVE)
Lt. William E. Babcock
51st New York Volunteers

(ABOVE)
Edward W. Flower
8th Michigan Volunteers

(BELOW)
Lt. James Watkins Mullery
15th New Jersey Volunteers

(BELOW)
George B. Field

Soldiers who gave Whitman their photographs as a remembrance.

(ABOVE)
Anson Rider, Jr.

(ABOVE)
Will W. Wallace

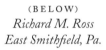

(BELOW)
Richard M. Ross
East Smithfield, Pa.

(BELOW)
Bethuel Smith
Glen's Falls, N.Y.

Part of Brandy Station, an encampment of the Union Army in northern Virginia in 1863. The stacked-up barrels are improvised chimneys.

Another view of Brandy Station, showing winter quarters being prepared for the 1st Connecticut Heavy Artillery. The soldier giving the salute seems to have been posing for the camera rather than showing respect for the officer on horseback.

*Whitman identified this photograph simply, but
significantly, as "Civil War soldier."*

174

Boys of 15, 16, 17, 18, are very common [in the army], middle-aged men rare.

175

…it was a dreadful night (last Friday night)—pretty dark, the wind gusty, and the rain fell in torrents. One poor boy—this is a sample of one case out of the 600—he seemed to be quite young, he was quite small (I looked at his body afterwards), he groaned some as the stretcher bearers were carrying him along, and again as they carried him through the hospital gate. They set down the stretcher and examined him, and the poor boy was dead. They took him into the ward, and the doctor came immediately, but it was all of no use. The worst of it is, too, that he is entirely unknown—there was nothing on his clothes, or any one with him to identify him, and he is altogether unknown…. It is enough to rack one's heart—such things. Very likely his folks will never know in the world what has become of him. Poor, poor child, for he appeared as though he could be but 18. I feel lately as though I must have some intermission. I feel well and hearty enough, and was never better, but my feelings are kept in a painful condition a great part of the time.

176

…when I see the common soldiers, what they go through, and how everybody seems to try to pick upon them, and what humbug there is over them every how, even the dying soldier's money stolen from his body by some scoundrel attendant, or from [the] sick one, even from under his head, which is a common thing, and then the agony I see every day, I get almost frightened at the world.

177

Gen. Grant has just come in town from front. The country here is all mad again. I am going to a spiritualist medium this evening—I expect it will be a humbug, of course.

APRIL

178

...I went to the see the great spirit medium, Foster. There were some little things some might call curious, perhaps, but it is a shallow thing and a humbug. A gentleman who was with me was somewhat impressed, but I could not see anything in it worth calling supernatural. I wouldn't turn on my heel to go again and see such things, or twice as much. We had table rappings and lots of nonsense.

179

April 7, 1864.—Walking down Pennsylvania Avenue.—Warmish forenoon, after the storm of the past few days. I see, passing up, in the broad space between the curbs, a big squad of a couple of hundred conscripts, surrounded by a strong cordon of arm'd guards, and others interspers'd between the ranks. The government has learn'd caution from its experiences; there are many hundreds of "bounty jumpers," and already, as I am told, eighty thousand deserters! Next (also passing up the Avenue,) a cavalry company, young, but evidently well drill'd and service-harden'd men. Mark the upright posture in their saddles, the bronz'd and bearded young faces, the easy swaying to the motions of the horses, and the carbines by their right knees; handsome and reckless, some eighty of them, riding with rapid gait, clattering along. Then the tinkling bells of passing cars, the many shops (some with large show-windows, some with swords, straps for the shoulders of different ranks, hat-cords with acorns, or other insignia,) the military patrol marching along, with the orderly or second-lieutenant stopping different ones to examine passes—the forms, the faces, all sorts crowded together, the worn and pale, the pleas'd, some on their way to the railroad depot going home, the cripples, the darkeys, the long trains of government wagons, or the sad strings of ambulances conveying wounded—the many officers' horses tied in front of the drinking or oyster saloons, or held by black men or boys, or orderlies.

There are exciting times in Congress—the Copperheads are getting furious and want to recognize the Southern Confederacy. This is a pretty time to talk of recognizing such villains after what they have done, and after what has transpired the last three years. After first Fredericksburg I felt discouraged myself, and doubted whether our rulers could carry on the war—but that has passed away. The war must be carried on, and I could willingly go myself in the ranks if I thought it would profit more than at present, and I don't know sometimes but I shall as it is.... You don't know what a feeling a man gets after being in the active sights and influences of the camp, the army, the wounded, etc. He gets to have a deep feeling he never experienced before—the flag, the tune of Yankee Doodle and similar things, produce an effect on a fellow never such before. I have seen some bring tears on the men's cheeks, and others turn pale, under such circumstances. I have a little flag; it belonged to one of our cavalry reg'ts; presented to me by one of the wounded. It was taken by the Secesh in a cavalry fight, and rescued by our men in a bloody little skirmish. It cost three men's lives, just to get one little flag, four by three. Our men rescued it, and tore it from the breast of a dead rebel—all that just for the name of getting their little banner back again. The man that got it was very badly wounded, and they let him keep it. I was with him a good deal; he wanted to give me something he said, he didn't expect to live, so he gave me the little banner as a keepsake.

I was up in Congress very late last night. The house had a very excited night session about expelling the men that want to recognize the Southern Confederacy. You ought to hear the soldiers talk. They are excited to madness. We shall probably have hot times here, not in the army alone. The soldiers are true as the North Star.

182

The Capitol grows upon one in time, especially as they have got the great figure on top of it now, and you can see it very well.

183

Washington
April 26, 1864

—Burnside's army passed through here yesterday. I saw George and walked with him in the regiment for some distance and had quite a talk. He is very well; he is very much tanned and looks hardy. I told him all the latest news from home. George stands it very well, and looks and behaves the same noble and good fellow he always was and always will be. It was on 14th st. I watched three hours before the 51st came along. I joined him just before they came to where the President and Gen. Burnside were standing with others on a balcony, and the interest of seeing me, etc., made George forget to notice the President and salute him. He was a little annoyed at forgetting it. I called his attention to it, but we had passed a little too far on, and George wouldn't turn round even ever so little. However, there was a great many more than half the army passed without noticing Mr. Lincoln and the others, for there was a great crowd all through the streets, especially here, and the place where the President stood was not conspicuous from the rest. The 9th Corps made a very fine show indeed. There were, I should think, five very full regiments of new black troops, under Gen. Ferrero. They looked and marched very well. It looked funny to see the President standing with his hat off to them just the same as the rest as they passed by. Then there [were the] Michigan regiments; one of them was a regiment of sharp-shooters, partly composed of Indians. Then there was a pretty strong force of artillery and a middling force of cavalry—many New York, Pennsylvania, Massachusetts, R.I., etc., reg'ts. All except the blacks were veterans [that had] seen plenty of fighting.... It is very different to see a real army of fighting men, from one of those shows in Brooklyn, or New York, or on Fort Greene.

...there was a powerful opposition to enlisting blacks during the earlier years of the secession war. Even then, however, they had their champions. "That the color'd race," said a good authority, "is capable of military training and efficiency, is demonstrated by the testimony of numberless witnesses, and by the eagerness display'd in the raising, organizing, and drilling of African troops. Few white regiments make a better appearance on parade than the First and Second Louisiana Native Guards. The same remark is true of other color'd regiments. At Milliken's Bend, at Vicksburg, at Port Hudson, on Morris Island, and wherever tested, they have exhibited determin'd bravery, and compell'd the plaudits alike of the thoughtful and thoughtless soldiery. During the siege of Port Hudson the question was often ask'd those who beheld their resolute charges, how the 'niggers' behav'd under fire; and without exception the answer was complimentary to them."

185

I haven't been out this morning and don't know what news—we know nothing, only that there is without doubt to be a terrible campaign here in Virginia this summer, and that all who know deepest about it are very serious about it.... It is serious times. I do not feel to fret or whimper, but in my heart and soul about our country, the forthcoming campaign with all its vicissitudes and the wounded and slain—I dare say... I feel the reality more than some because I am in the midst of its saddest results so much.

186

...I am now going down to see a poor soldier who is very low with a long diarrhoea—he cannot recover. When I was with him last night, he asked me before I went away to ask God's blessing on him. He says, I am no scholar and you are—poor dying man, I told him I hoped from the bottom of my heart God would bless him, and bring him up yet.

187

The difficulties of [President Lincoln's] situation have been unprecedented in the history of statesmanship. That he has conserved the government so far is a miracle itself. The difficulties have not been the south alone. The north has been & is yet honeycombed with semi-secesh sympathisers ever ready to undermine—& I am half disposed to predict that after the war closes, we shall see bevies of star-straps, two or three of our own Major Generals, shot for treachery, & fully deserve their fate.

188

As a very large proportion of the wounded came up from the front without a cent of money in their pockets, I soon discover'd that it was about the best thing I could do to raise their spirits, and show them that somebody cared for them, and practically felt a fatherly or brotherly interest in them, to give them small sums in such cases, using tact and discretion about it. I am regularly supplied with funds for this purpose by good women and men in Boston, Salem, Providence, Brooklyn, and New York.

MAY

189

The men like to have a pencil, and something to write in. I have given them cheap pocket-diaries, and almanacs for 1864, interleav'd with blank paper. For reading I generally have some old pictorial magazines or story papers—they are always acceptable. Also the morning or evening papers of the day. The best books I do not give, but lend to read through the wards, and then take them to others, and so on; they are very punctual about returning the books. In these wards, or on the field, as I thus continue to go round, I have come to adapt myself to each emergency, after its kind or call, however trivial, however solemn, every one justified and made real under its circumstances—not only visits and cheering talk and little gifts—not only washing and dressing wounds, (I have some cases where the patient is unwilling any one should do this but me)—but passages from the Bible, expounding them, prayer at the bedside, explanations of doctrine, &c. (I think I see my friends smiling at this confession, but I was never more in earnest in my life.) In camp and everywhere, I was in the habit of reading or giving recitations to the men. They were very fond of it, and liked declamatory poetical pieces. We would gather in a large group by ourselves, after supper, and spend the time in such readings, or in talking, and occasionally by an amusing game called the game of twenty questions.

190

The fighting down in the field on the 6th I think ended in our favor, though with pretty severe losses to some of our divisions. The fighting is about 70 miles from here, and 50 from Richmond—on the 7th and 8th followed up by the Rebel army hauling off, they say retreating, and Meade pursuing. It is quite mixed yet, but I guess we have the best of it. If we really have, Richmond is a goner, for they cannot do any better than they have done. The 9th Corps was in the fight, and where I cannot tell yet, but from the wounded I have seen I don't think that Corps was deeply in.

191

The poor diarrhoea man died, and it was a boon. Oscar Cunningham, 82nd Ohio, has had a relapse. I fear it is going bad with him. Lung diseases are quite plenty—night before last I staid in hospital all night tending a poor fellow. It has been awful hot here—milder to-day.

192

I have seen Col. LeGendre. He is here in Washington not far from where I am, 485 12th st. is his address. Poor man, I felt sorry indeed for him. He is badly wounded and disfigured. He is shot through the bridge of the nose, and left eye probably lost. I spent a little time with him this forenoon. He is suffering very much, spoke of George very kindly; said "Your brother is well." His orderly told me he saw him, George, Sunday night last, well.

193

May 23, '64.—Sometimes I think that should it come when it *must*, to fall in battle, one's anguish over a son or brother kill'd might be temper'd with much to take the edge off. Lingering and extreme suffering from wounds or sickness seem to me far worse than death in battle. I can honestly say the latter has no terrors for me, as far as I myself am concern'd. Then I should say, too, about death in war, that our feelings and imaginations make a thousand times too much of the whole matter. Of the many I have seen die, or known of, the past year, I have not seen or known one who met death with terror. In most cases I should say it was a welcome relief and release.

194

...I have changed my quarters—am at 502 Pennsylvania av., near 3d street, only a little way from the Capitol. Where I was, the house was sold and the old lady I hired the room from had to move out and give the owner possession. I like my new quarters pretty well—I have a room to myself, 3d story hall bedroom. I have my meals in the house.

195

—lately we have had the militia reg'ts pouring in here mostly from Ohio, they look first rate, I saw two or three come in yesterday, splendid American young men, from farms mostly—

196

Yesterday I spent a good part of the afternoon with a young soldier of seventeen, Charles Cutter, of Lawrence City, Massachusetts, 1st Massachusetts Heavy Artillery, Battery M. He was brought to one of the hospitals mortally wounded in abdomen. Well, I thought to myself, as I sat looking at him, it ought to be a relief to his folks if they could see how little he really suffer'd. He lay very placid, in a half lethargy, with his eyes closed. As it was extremely hot, and I sat a good while silently fanning him, and wiping the sweat, at length he open'd his eyes quite wide and clear, and look'd inquiringly around. I said, "What is it, my boy? Do you want anything?" He answer'd quietly, with a good-natured smile, "Oh, nothing; I was only looking around to see who was with me." His mind was somewhat wandering, yet he lay in an evident peacefulness that sanity and health might have envied. I had to leave for other engagements. He died, I heard afterward, without any special agitation, in the course of the night.

197

I often watch the city and environs from the roof of an elevated building near the Treasury.... Quite a good deal of house-building is in progress in one part of Washington and another.

198

...it is just the same old story, poor suffering young men, great swarms of them come up here, now, every day, all battered & bloody—there have 4000 arrived here this morning, & 1500 yesterday—

199

I wonder if I could ever convey to another— ...the tender and terrible realities of such cases... as the one I am now going to mention. Stewart C. Glover, company E, 5th Wisconsin—was wounded May 5, in one of those fierce tussles of the Wilderness—died May 21—aged about 20. He was a small and beardless young man—a splendid soldier—in fact almost an ideal American, of his age. He had serv'd nearly three years, and would have been entitled to his discharge in a few days. He was in Hancock's corps. The fighting had about ceas'd for the day, and the general commanding the brigade rode by and call'd for volunteers to bring in the wounded. Glover responded among the first—went out gayly—but while in the act of bearing in a wounded sergeant to our lines, was shot in the knee by a rebel sharp-shooter; consequence, amputation and death. He had resided with his father, John Glover, an aged and feeble man, in Batavia, Genesee county, N. Y., but was at school in Wisconsin, after the war broke out, and there enlisted—soon took to soldier-life, liked it, was very manly, was belov'd by officers and comrades. He kept a little diary, like so many of the soldiers. On the day of his death he wrote the following in it, *to-day the doctor says I must die—all is over with me—ah, so young to die.* On another blank leaf he pencill'd to his brother, *dear brother Thomas, I have been brave but wicked—pray for me.*

JUNE

200

...if this campaign was not in progress I should not stop here, as it is now beginning to tell a little upon me, so many bad wounds, many putrefied, and all kinds of dreadful one, I have been rather too much with—but as it is, I certainly remain here while the thing remains undecided. It is impossible for me to abstain from going to see and minister to certain cases, and that draws me into others, and so on. I have just left Oscar Cunningham, the Ohio boy—he is in a dying condition—there is no hope for him—it would draw tears from the hardest heart to look at him—he is all wasted away to a skeleton, and looks like some one fifty years old.... A year ago, when he was first brought in, I thought him the noblest specimen of a young Western man I had seen, a real giant in size, and always with a smile on his face. O what a change. He has long been very irritable to every one but me, and his frame is all wasted away.... The deaths in the principal hospital I visit, Armory-square, average one an hour.

201

...I gave the boys in Carver hospital a great treat of ice cream a couple of days ago, went round myself through about 15 large wards, (I bought some ten gallons, very nice)— ...many of the men had to be fed, several of them I saw cannot probably live, yet they quite enjoyed it, I gave everybody some—quite a number [of the] western country boys had never tasted ice cream before—they relish such things, oranges, lemons, &c— ...I feel a little blue this morning, as two young men I knew very well have just died, one died last night, & the other about half an hour before I went to the hospital, I did not anticipate the death of either of them, each was a very, very sad case, so young— ...I do not feel as first rate as usual—

202

I felt very much disturbed yesterday afternoon, as Major Hapgood came up from the paymaster general's office, and said that news had arrived that Burnside was killed, and that the 9th Corps had had a terrible slaughter. He said it was believed at the paymaster general's office. Well, I went out to see what reliance there was on it. The rumor soon spread over town, and was believed by many—but as near as I can make it out, it proves to be one of those unaccountable stories that get started these times. Saturday night we heard that Grant was routed completely, &c &c—so that's the way stories fly.... Well, the truth is sad enough, without adding anything to it—but Grant is not destroyed yet, but I think is going into Richmond yet, but the cost is terrible.... I have not felt well at all the last week. I had spells of deathly faintness and bad trouble in my head, too, and sore throat.... My head was the worst, though I don't know, the faint spells were not very pleasant—but I feel so much better this forenoon I believe it has passed over. There is a very horrible collection in Armory building, (in Armory-square hospital)—about 200 of the worst cases you ever see, and I had been probably too much with them. It is enough to melt the heart of a stone; over one third of them are amputation cases.... poor Oscar Cunningham is gone at last.... I was with him Saturday forenoon and also evening. He was more composed than usual, could not articulate very well. He died about 2 o'clock Sunday morning—very easy they told me. I was not there. It was a blessed relief; his life has been misery for months. The cause of death at last was the system absorbing the pus, the bad matter, instead of discharging it from [the] wound.... Things are going pretty badly with the wounded. They are crowded here in Washington in immense numbers, and all those that come up from the Wilderness and that region, arrived here so neglected, and in such plight, it was awful—(those that were at Fredericksburg and also from Ball Plain). The papers are full of puffs, etc., but the truth is, the largest proportion of worst cases got little or no attention. We receive them here with their wounds full of worms—some all swelled and inflamed. Many of the amputations have to be done over again. One new feature is that many of the poor afflicted young men are crazy. Every ward has some in it that are wandering. They have suffered too much, and it is perhaps a privilege that they are out of their senses.... It is most too much for a fellow, and I sometimes wish I was out of it—but I suppose it is because I have not felt first rate myself.... We get the wounded from our present field near Richmond much better than we did from the Wilderness and Fredericksburg. We get them now from White House. They are put on boats there, and come all the way here, about 160 or 170 miles. White House is only twelve or fifteen miles from the field, and is our present depot and base of supplies. It is very pleasant here to-day, a little cooler than it has been—a good rain shower last evening. The Western reg'ts continue to pour in here, the 100 days men;—many go down to front to guard posts, trains, &c.

...It seems to me if I could only be home two or three days, and have some good teas... and set in the old basement a while, and have a good time and talk with Jeff, and see the little girls, &c., I should be willing to keep on afterward among these sad scenes for the rest of the summer—but I shall remain here until this Richmond campaign is settled, anyhow, unless I get sick, and I don't anticipate that.

203

...I have not felt well again the last two days as I was Tuesday, but I feel a good deal better this morning. I go round, but most of the time feel very little like it. The doctor tells me I have continued too long in the hospitals, especially in a bad place, Armory building, where the worst wounds were, and have absorbed too much of the virus in my system—but I know it is nothing but what a little relief and sustenance of [the] right sort will set right. I am writing this in Major Hapgood's office. He is very busy paying off some men whose time is out; they are going home to New York.

204

I am not feeling very well these days—the doctors have told me not to come inside the hospitals for the present. I send there by a friend every day; I send things and aid to some cases I know, and hear from there also, but I do not go myself at present. It is probable that the hospital poison has affected my system, and I find it worse than I calculated. I have spells of faintness and very bad feeling in my head, fullness and pain—and besides sore throat.... But I shall feel better soon, I know—the doctors say it will pass over—they have long told me I was going in too strong. Some days I think it has all gone and I feel well again, but in a few hours I have a spell again.

205

Brooklyn
June 25 1864

...I got home all safe—I do not feel very well yet, but expect to, or begin to, pretty soon—

JULY

206

[Brooklyn]

The doctors say my sickness is from having too deeply imbibed poison into my system from the hospitals—I had spells of deathly faintness, & the disease also attacked my head & throat pretty seriously—

The doctors forbid me going any more into the hospitals—I did not think much of it, till I got pretty weak, & then they directed me to leave & go north for change of air as soon as I had strength—

207

Brooklyn
July 5, 1864

I have had three or four pretty bad days & nights—… my physician thinks that time, with the change of locality, & my own latent recuperative power, will make me well, but says my system is probably saturated with the virus of the hospitals &c which eludes ordinary treatment—&c &c &c…. I intend to move heaven & earth to publish my "Drum-Taps" as soon as I am able to go around.

208

Brooklyn
July 24, 1864

…I rec'd the volume of Navy Reports, transactions of iron clads, fights, &c. for '62 & '3—it will probably give me material for some pieces, thumb-nail sketches, for my *Drum-Taps*—

AUGUST

209

August 11 '64

Mother was telling me at dinner to-day, how glad she was when peace was declared after the War of 1812 &c. She said her father told them he hoped they never would be compelled to see the horrors of war, as he had seen them in the Revolution.

Mother's brothers were in the army at Brooklyn in 1812. She told me that her father came down to visit them & bring them some things, & she came with him. The camp must have been somewhere in the neighborhood of what is now Washington Park.

210

—after dinner in a knot of persons—W. W.—in a large group (among the rest, Dr. Vall, an army surgeon) passing away the time in telling anecdotes & stories, and a lady ask'd W. W. to tell something about his hospital experiences in the war—the conversation went on, in a somewhat desultory manner, without any thing specially memorable, until at length a lady who had not yet taken part in the conversation spoke up, "Mr. Whitman, I [have heard] it said that you formed many strong personal attachments in the army hospitals & met plenty of fine characters. Wont you tell us now, who perhaps most imprest you—who, perhaps, you loved the most, or took the strongest interest in."

The individual addressed paused a moment, looking at his questioner, and then said: Yes, I met in the hospitals the manliest & tenderest characters—I loved them all.

SEPTEMBER

211

Brooklyn
Sept 11 '64

My illness has passed over, & I go around the same as formerly, only a lingering suspicion of weakness now & then—I go out fishing & have been out riding frequently—

There is a hospital here, containing a couple hundred soldiers, it is only a quarter of a mile from our house, & I go there a good deal— am going this afternoon to spend the afternoon & evening—Strange

as it may seem days & days elapse without their having any visitors—
So… I am still in business—

212

…[at] the Brooklyn City Hospital, in Raymond-street, where I
found (taken in by contract) a number of wounded and sick from the
army. Most of the men were badly off, and without a cent of money,
many wanting tabacco. I supplied them, and a few special cases with
delicacies, also repeatedly with letter-paper, stamps, envelopes, &c.,
writing the addresses myself plainly, (a pleased crowd gathering
around me, as I directed for each one in turn.) This Brooklyn hospital is a bad place for soldiers, or anybody else. Cleanliness, proper
nursing, watching, &c., are more deficient than in any hospital I
know. For dinner on Sundays, I invariably found nothing but rice
and molasses. The men all speak well of Drs. Yale and Kissam for
kindness, patience, &c., and I think, from what I saw, they are also
skillful young medical men. But in its management otherwise, this is
the poorest hospital I have yet been in, out of many hundreds.

213

Br City hosp.

John C. Logan—Ward 27—Sept 3d '64—Co K—2d Penn Vol—
(shell wound inside rt leg between the knees & thigh, flesh torn
away—no bones fractured)— …at the Petersburg mine explosion—
came here about 6th Sept.—was better then than now—is but 17
years old, is from Pittsburgh—
　　Willard Beeman—Aged 21—83d Penn. in Brooklyn Hospital,
Sept 12—had a younger brother in same reg't, same company—is
uneasy about him, has not heard from him since last battle, though he
was in the habit of writing twice a week—they were most affectionate
brothers, always together, always loving, always true. "If it were to do
over again," said Willard, "I think I should rather enlist alone—the
feeling about my brother when going in a battle and anxiety about him
at other times, is more than I can stand."—There were six of these
Beemans, wagon makers, in Pennsylvania—five of them have been or

are in the army. One of the five is dead. The parents are not living.

214

I go out quite regularly, sometimes out on the bay, or to Coney Island—& occasionally a tour through New York life, as of old—last night I was with some of my friends of Fred Gray association, till late wandering the east side of the City—first in the lager bier saloons & then elsewhere—one crowded, low, most degraded place we went, a poor blear-eyed girl bringing beer. I saw her with a McClellan medal on her breast—I called her & asked her if the other girls there were for McClellan too—she said yes every one of them, & that they wouldn't tolerate a girl in the place who was not, & *the fellows* were too—(there must have been twenty girls, sad sad ruins)—it was one of those places where the air is full of the scent of low thievery, druggies, foul play, & prostitution gangrened—

215

I don't know what move I shall make, but something soon, as it is not satisfactory any more in New York & Brooklyn—I should think nine tenths, of all classes, are copperheads here, I never heard before such things as I hear now whenever I go out—then it seems tame & indeed unreal here, life as carried on & as I come in contact with it & receive its influences—

216

We felt pretty gloomy some little time since, as two young men of the 51st N Y, friends of my brother George & of our family (officers of 51st), were killed in battle within ten days of each other & their bodies brought on for burial here—Mother was at the funeral of each of them, & I also—the regiment is on the Weldon road & in a position of danger—

OCTOBER

217

Brooklyn
Oct 8 '64

I am pretty well, perhaps not so unconsciously hearty as before my sickness—We are deprest in spirits [about George]—if not killed, he is a prisoner—he was in the engagement of Sept 30 on the extreme left.

218

The political meetings in New York & Brooklyn are immense—I go to them as to shows, fireworks, cannon, clusters of gaslights, countless torches, banners & mottos, 15, 20, 50,000 people—Per contra I occasionally go riding off in the country, in quiet lanes, or a sail on the water, & many times to the sea shore at Coney Island—

NOVEMBER

219

[Brooklyn]

...in an engagement (the papers have called it battle of Poplar Grove,) on the extreme left, toward the evening of the 30th of September, the Fifty-first had the bad luck to be captured almost entire. Our men, in considerable strength, (two divisions Ninth Corps, and two Fifth Corps, with some cavalry,) stretched out in the forenoon from the left, intending an endeavor toward the southerly of the two railroads running from the enemy's region directly to Burkeville. We met with some success at first at PEEBLE's farm, but about five o'clock in the afternoon the Second Division, Ninth Corps, in advance, encountered strong rebel works on an acclivity, up which they

attempted to press, but were repulsed. The secesh troops, being rein-
forced and sallying down, in turn attacked us. Their charge was
vehement, and caused that part of our force on the right of the Fifty-
first to give way, whereupon the enemy rapidly throwing a powerful
flanking column through the gap this made, completed the disaster
by cutting off the Fifty-first and some other troops, who formed the
extreme left, and after a sharp tussel capturing them, under circumstances honorable to the regiment. There were ten companies captured, of from 30 to 40 men each, and the following officers: Maj.
John G. Wright, Acting Colonel; Capt. George W. Whitman, Acting Lieutenant-Colonel; [and twelve others].

220

[Brooklyn]

I have lately been (Nov. 25) in the Central Park Hospital, near One
Hundred and Fourth-street. It seems to be a well-managed institution.

DECEMBER

221

[Brooklyn]

...I intend returning to Washington this winter—I do not know
how soon.... Mother remains well, & in pretty good spirits, better
than I would have expected—[George] remains a prisoner—as near
as we can judge he is at Columbia, S C—we have had no word from
him—

222

Monday night December 26, 1864. I am writing this in the front
basement in Portland Avenue, Brooklyn, at home. It is after 9
o'clock at night. We have had a wet day with fog, mud, slush, and

the yet unmelted hard polished ice liberally left in the streets. All sluggish and damp, with a prevailing leaden vapor. Yesterday, Christmas, about the same. George's trunk came by express today early in the forenoon from City Point, Virginia. Lt. Babcock, of the 51st was kind enough to search it out & send it home. It stood some hours before we felt inclined to open it. Towards evening Mother and Eddy looked over the things. One could not help feeling depressed. There were his uniform coat, pants, sash, &c. There were many things reminded us of him. Papers, memoranda, books, nicknacks, a revolver, a small diary, roll of his company, a case of photographs of his comrades (several of them I knew as killed in battle) with other stuff such as a soldier accumulates. Mother looked everything over[,] laid out the shirts to be washed, the coats and pants to hang up, & all the rest were carefully put back. It made us feel pretty solemn. We have not heard from him since October 3rd; whether living or dead we know not. I am aware of the condition of the union prisoners south, through seeing them when brought up, & from lately talking with a friend just returned from taking part in the exchange at Savannah and Charleston by which we have received 12,000 of our sick. Their situation, as of all men in prison, is indescribably horrible.

223

The public mind is deeply excited, and most righteously so, at the starvation of the United States prisoners of war in the hands of the Secessionists. The dogged sullenness and scoundrelism prevailing everywhere among the prison guards and officials, (with, I think, the general exception of the surgeons,) the measureless torments of the forty or fifty thousand helpless young men, with all their humiliations, hunger, cold, filth, despair, hope utterly given out, and the more and more frequent imbecility, I have myself seen the proofs of in so many instances, that I know the facts well, and know that the half has not been told, nor the tithe either….

…considerably more than one-fourth of those helpless and most wretched men, (their last hours passed in the thought that they were abandoned by their Government, and left to their fate,) have been exchanged by deaths of starvation... leaving half the remainder closely to prepare to follow, from mental and physical atrophy; and even the remnant cannot long tarry behind.

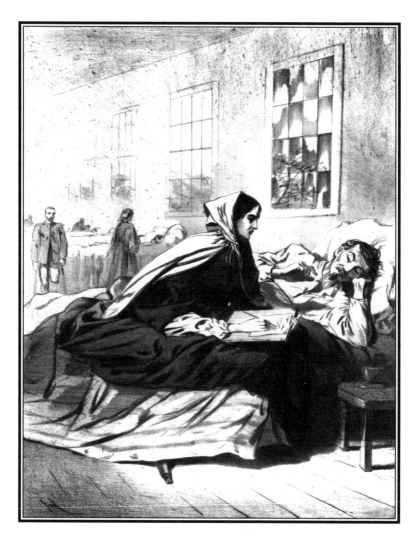

"The Letter for Home," a lithograph by Winslow Homer.

Third Year of Service, 1865

THE DRESSER.

—

1 An old man bending, I come, among new faces,
Years looking backward, resuming, in answer to chil-
    dren,
Come tell us old man, as from young men and maidens
    that love me ;
Years hence of these scenes, of these furious passions,
    these chances,
Of unsurpass'd heroes, (was one side so brave ? the
    other was equally brave ;)
Now be witness again — paint the mightiest armies of
    earth ;
Of those armies so rapid, so wondrous, what saw you to
    tell us ?
What stays with you latest and deepest ? of curious
    panics,
Of hard-fought engagements, or sieges tremendous,
    what deepest remains ?

2 O maidens and young men I love, and that love me,
What you ask of my days, those the strangest and sud-
    den your talking recals ;
Soldier alert I arrive, after a long march, cover'd with
    sweat and dust ;
In the nick of time I come, plunge in the fight, loudly
    shout in the rush of successful charge ;
Enter the captur'd works . . . . yet lo ! like a swift-
    running river, they fade ;
Pass and are gone, they fade — I dwell not on soldiers'
    perils or soldiers' joys ;
(Both I remember well — many the hardships, few the
    joys, yet I was content.)

(31)

A page from "Drum-Taps."

Brooklyn January 6 1865

IT MAY BE DRUM-TAPS may come out this winter, yet, (in the way I have mentioned in times past.) It is in a state to put right through, a perfect copy being ready for the printers—I feel at last, & for the first time without any demur, that I am satisfied with it—content to have it go to the world verbatim & punctuation.... I am perhaps mainly satisfied with Drum-Taps because it delivers my ambition of the task that has haunted me, namely, to express in a poem (& in the way I like, which is not at all by directly stating it) the pending action of this *Time & Land we swim in,* with all their large conflicting fluctuations of despair & hope, the shiftings, masses, & the whirl & deafening din, (yet over all, as by invisible hand, a definite purport & idea)—with the unprecedented anguish of wounded & suffering, the beautiful young men, in wholesale death & agony, everything sometimes as if in blood color, & dripping blood. The book is therefore unprecedently sad, (as these days are, are they not?)—but it also has the blast of the trumpet, & the drum pounds & whirrs in it, & then an undertone of sweetest comradeship & human love, threading its steady thread inside the chaos, & heard at every lull & interstice thereof—truly also it has clear notes of faith & triumph.

225

Not a word for over three months from my brother George—the probabilities are most gloomy.

Washington

To-night I have been wandering awhile in the capitol, which is all lit up. The illuminated rotunda looks fine. I like to stand aside and look a long, long while, up at the dome; it comforts me somehow. The House and Senate were both in session till very late. I look'd in upon them, but only a few moments; they were hard at work on tax and appropriation bills. I wander'd through the long and rich corridors and apartments under the Senate; an old habit of mine, former winters, and now more satisfaction than ever. Not many persons down there, occasionally a flitting figure in the distance.

As I walk'd home about sunset, I saw in Fourteenth street a very young soldier, thinly clad, standing near the house I was about to enter. I stopt a moment in front of the door and call'd him to me. I knew that an old Tennessee regiment, and also an Indiana regiment, were temporarily stopping in new barracks, near Fourteenth street. This boy I found belonged to the Tennessee regiment. But I could hardly believe he carried a musket. He was but 15 years old, yet had been twelve months a soldier, and had borne his part in several battles, even historic ones. I ask'd him if he did not suffer from the cold, and if he had no overcoat. No, he did not suffer from cold, and had no overcoat, but could draw one whenever he wish'd. His father was dead, and his mother living in some part of East Tennessee; all the men were from that part of the country. The next forenoon I saw the Tennessee and Indiana regiments marching down the Avenue. My boy was with the former, stepping along with the rest. There were many other boys no older. I stood and watch'd them as they tramp'd along with slow, strong, heavy, regular steps. There did not appear to be a man over 30 years of age, and a large proportion were from 15 to perhaps 22 or 23. They had all the look of veterans, worn, stain'd, impassive, and a certain unbent, lounging gait, carrying in addition to their regular arms and knapsacks, frequently a frying-pan, broom, &c.

Sunday... Pass'd this afternoon among a collection of unusually bad cases, wounded and sick Secession soldiers, left upon our hands. I spent the previous Sunday afternoon there also. At that time two were dying. Two others have died during the week. Several of them are partly deranged. I went around among them elaborately. Poor boys, they all needed to be cheer'd up. As I sat down by any particular one, the eyes of all the rest in the neighboring cots would fix upon me, and remain steadily riveted as long as I sat within their sight. Nobody seem'd to wish anything special to eat or drink. The main thing ask'd for was postage stamps, and paper for writing. I distributed all the stamps I had. Tobacco was wanted by some.

One call'd me over to him and ask'd me in a low tone what denomination I belong'd to. He said he was a Catholic—wish'd to find some one of the same faith—wanted some good reading. I gave him something to read, and sat down by him a few minutes. Moved around with a word for each. They were hardly any of them personally attractive cases, and no visitors come here. Of course they were all destitute of money. I gave small sums to two or three, apparently the most needy. The men are from quite all the Southern States, Georgia, Mississippi, Louisiana, &c.

The large ward I am in is used for Secession soldiers exclusively. One man, about forty years of age, emaciated with diarrhoea, I was attracted to, as he lay with his eyes turn'd up, looking like death. His weakness was so extreme that it took a minute or so, every time, for him to talk with anything like consecutive meaning; yet he was evidently a man of good intelligence and education. As I said anything, he would lie a moment perfectly still, then, with closed eyes, answer in a low, very slow voice, quite correct and sensible, but in a way and tone that wrung my heart. He had a mother, wife, and child living (or probably living) in his home in Mississippi. It was long, long since he had seen them. Had he caus'd a letter to be sent them since he got here in Washington? No answer. I repeated the question, very slowly and soothingly. He could not tell whether he had or not—things of late seem'd to him like a dream. After waiting a moment, I said: "Well, I am going to walk down the ward a moment, and when I come back you can tell me. If you have not written, I will sit down and write." A few minutes after I return'd; he said he remember'd now that some one had written for him two or three days before. The presence of this man impress'd me profoundly. The flesh was all sunken on face and arms; the eyes low in their sockets and glassy, and with purple rings around them. Two or three great tears silently flow'd out from the eyes, and roll'd down his temples (he was doubtless unused to be spoken to as I was speaking to him.) Sickness, imprisonment, exhaustion, &c., had conquer'd the body, yet the mind held mastery still, and call'd even wandering remembrance back.

There are some fifty Southern soldiers here; all sad, sad, cases. There is a good deal of scurvy.

230

Wrote several letters. One for a young fellow named Thomas J. Byrd, with a bad wound and diarrhoea. Was from Russell county, Alabama; been out four years. Wrote to his mother; had neither heard from her nor written to her in nine months. Was taken prisoner last Christmas, in Tennessee; sent to Nashville, then to Camp Chase, Ohio, and kept there a long time; all the while not money enough to get paper and postage stamps. Was paroled, but on his way home the wound took gangrene; had diarrhoea also; had evidently been very low. Demeanor cool, and patient. A dark-skinn'd, quaint young fellow, with strong Southern idiom; no education.

Another letter for John W. Morgan, aged 18, from Shellot, Brunswick county, North Carolina; been out nine months; gunshot wound in right leg, above knee; also diarrhoea; wound getting along well; quite a gentle, affectionate boy; wish'd me to put in the letter for his mother to kiss his little brother and sister for him. I put strong envelopes on these, and two or three other letters, directed them plainly and fully, and dropt them in the Washington post-office the next morning myself.

Washington, D. C.
January 30 '65

I am quite comfortable, have a comfortable room enough, with a
wood stove, & a pile of wood in the room, a first rate & good big bed,
& a very friendly old secesh landlady whose husband & son are off
in the Southern army—she is different from any I have found yet
here, is very obliging, starts my fire for me at 5 o'clock every afternoon, & lights the gas, even, & then turns it down to be ready for me
when I come home.

[I now have a job in] the Indian Office—it is a Bureau in the Department of the Interior, which has charge of quite a large mass of business relating to the numerous Indian tribes in West and Northwest,
large numbers of whom are under annuities, supplies, &c. from the
government. All I have hitherto employed myself about has been
making copies of reports and bids &c. for the office to send up to the
Congressional Committee on Indian Affairs.—It is easy enough—I
take things very easy—the rule is to come at 9, and go at 4—but I
don't come at 9, and only stay till 4 when I want....

FEBRUARY

Washington
February 4 1865

I spend a portion of my time around among the Hospitals as formerly—I find quite a good many bad old lingering wounds, & also a
good many down with sickness of one sort or another—& the latter
are receiving accessions every day—especially as they appear to be
breaking up the Corps Hospitals in front, down in Grant's army—a

good many of the men have been sent up here—day before yesterday I saw a string of over a hundred ambulances, bringing up the men from the depot, to distribute them around to the different Hospitals.

My heath is pretty good, & I remain in good spirits considering.

I have a little employment here, of three or four hours every day. It is regular, & sufficiently remunerative—Sundays I spend most of the day in the Hospitals—during the week a few hours from time to time, & occasionally in the evening.

234

Since I was prostrated last July, I have not had that unconscious and perfect health I formerly had. The physician says my system has been penetrated by the malaria—it is tenacious, peculiar and somewhat baffling—but tells me it will go over in due time. It is my first appearance in the character of a man not entirely well.

235

Michael Stansbury, 48 years of age, a sea-faring man, a southerner by birth and raising, formerly captain of U. S. light ship Long Shoal, station'd at Long Shoal point, Pamlico sound—though a southerner, a firm Union man—was captur'd Feb. 17, 1863, and has been nearly two years in the Confederate prisons; was at one time order'd releas'd by Governor Vance, but a rebel officer re-arrested him; then sent on to Richmond for exchange—but instead of being exchanged was sent down (as a southern citizen, not a soldier,) to Salisbury, N. C., where he remain'd until lately, when he escap'd among the exchang'd by assuming the name of a dead soldier, and coming up via Wilmington with the rest. Was about sixteen months in Salisbury. Subsequent to October, '64, there were about 11,000 Union prisoners in the stockade; about 100 of them southern unionists, 200 U. S. deserters. During the past winter 1500 of the prisoners, to save their lives, join'd the confederacy, on condition of being assign'd merely to guard duty. Out of the 11,000 not more than 2500 came out.... Has seen men brought there to Salisbury as hearty as you ever see in your life—in a few weeks completely dead gone, much of it from thinking on their condition—hope all gone. Has himself a hard, sad, strangely dead-en'd kind of look, as of one chill'd for years in the cold and dark, where his good manly nature had no room to exercise itself.

236

...I steadily found more and more, that I could help and turn the balance in favor of cure, by [affection and personal attention], in a curiously large proportion of cases. The American soldier is full of affection, and the yearning for affection. And it comes wonderfully grateful to him to have this yearning gratified when he is laid up with painful wounds or illness, far away from home, among strangers. Many will think this merely sentimentalism, but I know it is the most solid of facts. I believe that even the moving around among the men, or through the ward, of a hearty, healthy, clean, strong, generous-souled person, man or woman, full of humanity and love, sending out invisible, constant currents therof, does immense good to the sick and wounded.

237

...each case requires some peculiar adaptation to itself. It is very important to slight nobody—not a single case. Some hospital visitors, especially the women, pick out the handsomest looking soldiers, or have a few for their pets. Of course some will attract you more than others, and some will need more attention than others; but be careful not to ignore any patient. A word, a friendly turn of the eye, or touch of the hand in passing, if nothing more.

238

I write this in my room in Washington. A heavy sulky night, & beating snow storm. I have just opened the window and looked out. It is bleak and silent and dim. Off in a distant camp the drums beat tattoos, and in a neighboring hospital the long-drawn bugle notes give the same signal.

239

Washington
Feb. 27, 1865

Why did not [George], & the other officers, 51st N. Y., come up with
the main body, for exchange?

240

This city, its suburbs, the capitol, the front of the White House, the
places of amusement, the Avenue, and all the main streets, swarm
with soldiers this winter, more than ever before. Some are out from
the hospitals, some from the neighboring camps, &c. One source or
another, they pour plenteously, and make, I should say, the mark'd
feature in the human movement and costume-appearance of our
national city. Their blue pants and overcoats are everywhere....
Toward the latter part of the afternoon, you see the furlough'd men,
sometimes singly, sometimes in small squads, making their way to
the Baltimore depot. At all times, except early in the morning, the
patrol detachments are moving around, especially during the earlier
hours of evening, examining passes, and arresting all soldiers without them. They do not question the one-legged, or men badly dis-
abled or maim'd, but all others are stopt. They also go around
evenings through the auditoriums of the theatres, and make officers
and all show their passes, or other authority, for being there.

241

...in a hospital corner... a dying Irish boy, a Catholic priest, and an
improvised altar—

242

There is certainly not one government in Europe but is now watch-
ing the war in this country, with the ardent prayer that the United
States may be effectually split, crippled, and dismember'd by it.
There is not one but would help toward dismemberment, if it dared.
I say such is the ardent wish to-day of England and of France, as

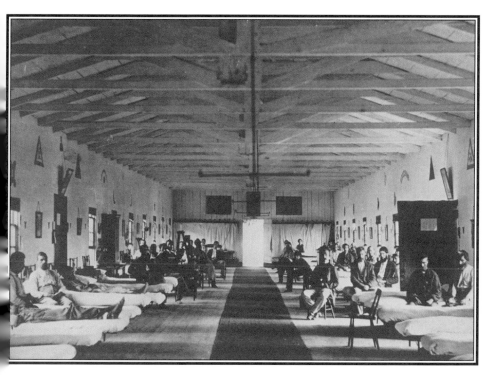

Ward K, Armory Square Hospital, Washington:
the hospital Whitman visited most frequently.

One of the tent hospitals set up to handle the massive volumes of sick and wounded brought to Washington from the nearby war zone.

Stanton Hospital, where Whitman encountered
numerous Confederate patients in the
last year of the war.

ABOVE: *Hospital stewards, 2nd Division, 9th Corps. The 51st New York Volunteers, George Whitman's regiment, was part of this corps.*

BELOW: *Surgeons at Finlay Hospital, Washington.*

ABOVE: *Quartermaster's Hospital, one of the fifty military hospitals established in Washington during the Civil War.*

BELOW: *Campbell Hospital.*

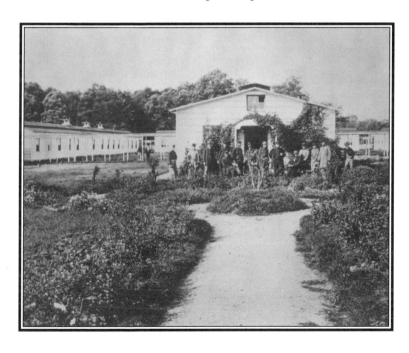

Harewood Hospital, the last of the military hospitals to close in 1866.

Ward in Harewood Hospital

Whitman in 1867

governments, and of all the nations of Europe, as governments. I think indeed it is to-day the real, heartfelt wish of all the nations of the world, with the single exception of Mexico—Mexico, the only one to whom we have ever really done wrong, and now the only one who prays for us and for our triumph, with genuine prayer. Is it not indeed strange? America, made up of all, cheerfully from the beginning opening her arms to all, the result and justifier of all, of Britain, Germany, France and Spain—all here—the accepter, the friend, hope, last resource and general house of all—she who has harm'd none, but been bounteous to so many, to millions, the mother of strangers and exiles, all nations—should now I say be paid this dread compliment of general governmental fear and hatred. Are we indignant? alarm'd? Do we feel jeopardized? No; help'd, braced, concentrated, rather. We are all too prone to wander from ourselves, to affect Europe, and watch her frowns and smiles. We need this hot lesson of general hatred, and henceforth must never forget it. Never again will we trust the moral sense nor abstract friendliness of a single *government* of the old world.

MARCH

243

Plenty more butternut or clay-color'd escapees every day. About 160 came in to-day, a large portion South Carolinians. They generally take the oath of allegiance, and are sent north, west, or extreme south-west if they wish. Several of them told me that the desertions in their army, of men going home, leave or no leave, are far more numerous than their desertions to our side. I saw a very forlorn looking squad of about a hundred, late this afternoon, on their way to the Baltimore depot.

244

One hardly supposed there were so many mules in the Western

world as you see these times about Washington and everywhere in the military camps, little and large, through Virginia. Saturday forenoon last on K street, moving up, I saw an immense drove of mules, I should think towards two thousand, and most of them very fine animals. Three or four horsemen went just ahead, with peculiar cries that seemed to have a kind of charm over the creatures, for those along the front part of the drove followed the shouting horsemen implicitly, and thus the great mass were drawn resistlessly on. Other horsemen—a score of them—dashed athwart the sides, whipping in the stragglers; but it was remarkable to me how such a great mule army in motion kept together with so little perversity and off-shooting.

245

I have been up to look at the dance and supper-rooms, for the inauguration ball at the Patent office; and I could not help thinking, what a different scene they presented to my view a while since, fill'd with a crowded mass of the worst wounded of the war, brought in from second Bull Run, Antietam, and Fredericksburgh. To-night, beautiful women, perfumes, the violins' sweetness, the polka and the waltz; then the amputation, the blue face, the groan....

246

I must mention a strange scene at the capitol, the hall of Representatives, the morning of Saturday last, (March 4th.) The day just dawn'd, but in half-darkness, everything dim, leaden, and soaking. In that dim light, the members nervous from long drawn duty, exhausted, some asleep, and many half asleep. The gas-light, mix'd with the dingy day-break, produced an unearthly effect. The poor little sleepy, stumbling, pages, the smell of the hall, the members with heads leaning on their desks, the sounds of the voices speaking, with unusual intonations—the general moral atmosphere also of the close of this important session—the strong hope that the war is approaching its close—the tantalizing dread lest the hope may be a false one—the grandeur of the hall itself, with its effect of vast shadows up toward the panels and spaces over the galleries—all made a mark'd combination.

In the midst of this, with the suddenness of a thunderbolt, burst one of the most angry and crashing storms of rain and hail ever heard. It beat like a deluge on the heavy glass roof of the hall, and the wind literally howl'd and roar'd. For a moment, (and no wonder,) the nervous and sleeping Representatives were thrown into a confusion. The slumberers awaked with fear, some started for the doors, some look'd up with blanch'd cheeks and lips to the roof, and the little pages began to cry; it was a scene. But it was over almost as soon as the drowsied men were actually awake. They recover'd themselves; the storm raged on, beating, dashing, and with loud noises at times. But the House went ahead with its business then, I think, as calmly and with as much deliberation as at any time in its career. Perhaps the shock did it good. (One is not without impression, after all, amid these members of Congress, of both the Houses, that if the flat routine of their duties should ever be broken in upon by some great emergency involving real danger, and calling for first-class personal qualities, those qualities would be found generally forthcoming, and from men not now credited with them.)

247

We all know the chorus: Washington, dusty, muddy, tiresome Washington is the most awful place, political and other; it is the rendezvous of the national universal axe-grinding, caucusing, and of our never-ending ballot-chosen shysters, and perennial smouchers, windy bawlers from every quarter far and near.... This city, concentre to-day of the inauguration of the new adjustment of the civilized world's political power and geography, with vaster consequences of Presidential and Congressional action; things done here, these days, bearing on the status of man, long centuries; the spot and the hour here making history's basic materials and widest ramifications; the city of the armies of the good old cause, full of significant signs, surrounded with weapons and armaments on every hill as I look forth, and THE FLAG flying over it all. The city that launches the direct laws, the imperial laws of American Union and Democracy, to be henceforth compelled, when needed, at the point of the bayonet and the muzzle of cannon—launched over continental areas, three millions of square miles, an empire large as Europe. The city of wounded and sick, city of hospitals, full of the sweetest, bravest children of time or lands; tens of thousands, wounded, bloody, amputated, burning with fever, blue with diarrhoea. The city of the wide Potomac, the queenly river, lined with softest, greenest hills and uplands. The city of Congress, with debates, agitations, (petty, if you please, but full of future fruit,) of chaotic formings; of Congress knowing not itself, as it sits there in its rooms of gold, knowing not the depths of consequence belonging to it, that lie below the scum and eructations of its surface.

But where am I running to? I meant to make a few observations of Washington on the surface.

248

I ought to make mention of the closing levee of Saturday night last. Never before was such a compact jam in front of the White House—all the grounds fill'd, and away out to the spacious sidewalks. I was there, as I took a notion to go—was in the rush inside with the crowd—surged along the passage-ways, the blue and other rooms, and through the great east room. Crowds of country people, some very funny. Fine music from the Marine band, off in a side place. I saw Mr. Lincoln, drest all in black, with white kid gloves and a claw-hammer coat, receiving, as in duty bound, shaking hands, looking very disconsolate, and as if he would give anything to be somewhere else.

249

J. H. G., bed 24, wants an undershirt, drawers, and socks; has not had a change for quite a while; is evidently a neat, clean boy from New England—(I supplied him; also with a comb, tooth-brush, and some soap and towels; I noticed afterward he was the cleanest of the whole ward.) Mrs. G., lady-nurse, ward F, wants a bottle of brandy—has two patients imperatively requiring stimulus—low with wounds and exhaustion. (I supplied her with a bottle of first-rate brandy from the Christian commission rooms.)

250

Here is an incident just occurr'd in one of the hospitals. A lady named Miss or Mrs. Billings, who has long been a practical friend of soldiers, and nurse in the army, and had become attached to it in a way that no one can realize but him or her who has had experience, was taken sick, early this winter, linger'd some time, and finally died in the hospital. It was her request that she should be buried among the soldiers, and after the military method. This request was fully carried out. Her coffin was carried to the grave by soldiers, with the usual escort, buried, and a salute fired over the grave.

251

There are many women in one position or another, among the hospitals, mostly as nurses here in Washington, and among the military stations; quite a number of them young ladies acting as volunteers. They are a help in certain ways, and deserve to be mention'd with respect. Then it remains to be distinctly said that few or no young ladies, under the irresistible conventions of society, answer the practical requirements of nurses for soldiers. Middle-aged or healthy and good condition'd elderly women, mothers of children, are always best. Many of the wounded must be handled. A hundred things which cannot be gainsay'd, must occur and must be done. The presence of a good middle-aged or elderly woman, the magnetic touch of hands, the expressive features of the mother, the silent soothing of her presence, her words, her knowledge and privileges arrived at only through having had children, are precious and final qualifications. It is a natural faculty that its required; it is not merely having a genteel young woman at a table in a ward. One of the finest nurses I met was a red-faced illiterate old Irish woman; I have seen her take the poor wasted naked boys so tenderly up in her arms.

252

Brooklyn
March 26, 1865

Both my mother & brother George looked much better than expected— ... [He] would be in what I would almost call fair condition, if it were not that his legs are affected—it seems to me it is rheumatism, following the fever he had—but I don't know—He goes to bed quite sleepy & falls to sleep—but then soon wakes, & frequently little or no more sleep that night—he most always leaves the bed, & comes downstairs, & passes the night on the sofa. He goes out most every day though—some days has to lay by—He is going to report to Annapolis promptly when his furlough is up—I told him I had no doubt I could get it extended, but he does not wish it—He says little, but is in first rate spirits.

I am feeling finely—& never enjoyed a visit home more than I am doing this.

I find myself perplexed about printing my book [*Drum-Taps*]. All the printers tell me I could not pick a more inopportune time— that in ten days prices of paper, composition &c will all be very much lower &c. I shall decide to-morrow.

APRIL

253

Brooklyn
April 7, 1865

I am stopping longer than first intended, as I have decided to print the book, and am now under way with it. Probably I will not be back [in Washington] till 16th or 17th.

254

Lincoln's death— thousands of flags at half mast—& on numbers of

them long black pennants—from the shipping densely crowding the
docks, the same—numerous boats constantly plying across the river,
the same solemn signal—black—business public & private all suspended, & the shops closed—strange mixture of horror, fury, tenderness, & a stirring of wonder brewing.

255

All Broadway is black with mourning—the facades of the houses are
festooned with black—great flags with wide & heavy fringes of dead
black, give a pensive effect—towards noon the sky darkened & it
began to rain. Drip, drip, & heavy moist black weather—the stores
are all closed—the rain sent the women from the street & black
clothed men only remained—black clouds driving overhead—the
horror, fever, uncertainty, alarm in the public—Every hour brings a
great history event on the wires—at 11 o'clock the new president is
sworn—

256

Mother prepared breakfast—and other meals afterwards—as usual;
but not a mouthful was eaten all day by either of us. We each drank
half a cup of coffee; that was all. Little was said. We got every newspaper morning and evening, and the frequent extras of that period,
and pass'd them silently to each other.

257

I shall not easily forget the first time I ever saw Abraham Lincoln. It
must have been about the 18th or 19th of February, 1861. It was rather
a pleasant afternoon, in New York city, as he arrived there from the
West, to remain a few hours, and then pass on to Washington, to prepare for his inauguration. I saw him in Broadway, near the site of the
present Post-office. He came down, I think from Canal street, to stop
at the Astor House. The broad spaces, sidewalks, and street in the
neighborhood, and for some distance, were crowded with solid
masses of people, many thousands. The omnibuses and other vehicles

had all been turn'd off, leaving an unusual hush in that busy part of the city. Presently two or three shabby hack barouches made their way with some difficulty through the crowd, and drew up at the Astor House entrance. A tall figure step'd out of the centre of these barouches, paus'd leisurely on the sidewalk, look'd up at the granite walls and looming architecture of the grand old hotel—then, after a relieving stretch of arms and legs, turn'd round for over a minute to slowly and good-humoredly scan the appearance of the vast and silent crowds. There were no speeches—no compliments—no welcome— as far as I could hear, not a word said. Still much anxiety was conceal'd in that quiet. Cautious persons had fear'd some mark'd insult or indignity to the President-elect—for he possess'd no personal popularity at all in New York city, and very little political. But it was evidently tacitly agreed that if the few political supporters of Mr. Lincoln present would entirely abstain from any demonstration on their side, the immense majority, who were any thing but supporters, would abstain on their side also. The result was a sulky, unbroken silence, such as certainly never before characterized so great a New York crowd.

Almost in the same neighborhood I distinctly remember'd seeing Lafayette on his visit to America in 1825. I had also personally seen and hear, various years afterward, how Andrew Jackson, Clay, Webster, Hungarian Kossuth, Filibuster Walker, the Prince of Wales on his visit, and other celebres, native and foreign, had been welcom'd there—all that indescribable human roar and magnetism, unlike any other sound in the universe—the glad exulting thunder-shouts of countless unloos'd throats of men! But on this occasion, not a voice—not a sound. From the top of an omnibus, (driven up one side, close by, and block'd by the curbstone and the crowds,) I had, I say, a capital view of it all, and especially of Mr. Lincoln, his look and gait—his perfect composure and coolness—his unusual and uncouth height, his dress of complete black, stovepipe hat push'd back on the head, dark-brown complexion, seam'd and wrinkled yet canny-looking face, black, bushy head of hair, disproportionately long neck, and his hands held behind as he stood observing the people. He look'd with curiosity upon that immense sea of faces, and the sea of faces return'd the look with similar curiosity. In both there was a dash of comedy, almost farce, such as Shakspere puts in his blackest tragedies. The crowd that hemm'd around consisted I should think of thirty to forty thousand men, not a single one his personal friend—while I have no doubt, (so frenzied were the ferments of the time,) many an assassin's knife and pistol lurk'd in hip or breast-pocket there, ready, soon as break and riot came.

But no break or riot came. The tall figure gave another relieving stretch or two of arms and legs; then with moderate pace, and accompanied by a few unknown looking persons, ascended the por-tico-steps of the Astor House, disappear'd through its broad entrance—and the dumb-show ended.

258

Washington, D.C.

The western star, Venus, in the earlier hours of evening, has never been so large, so clear; it seems as if it told something, as if it held rapport indulgent with humanity, with us Americans. Five or six nights since, it hung close by the moon, then a little past its first quarter. The star was wonderful, the moon like a young mother. The sky, dark blue, the transparent night, the planets, the moderate west wind, the elastic temperature, the miracle of that great star, and the young and swelling moon swimming in the west, suffused the soul. Then I heard, slow and clear, the deliberate notes of a bugle come up out of the silence, sounding so good through the night's mystery, no hurry, but firm and faithful, floating along, rising, falling leisurely, with here and there a long-drawn note; the bugle, well play'd, sound-ing tattoo, in one of the army hospitals near here, where the wounded (some of them personally so dear to me,) are lying in their cots....

259

...[at the time of Lincoln's death] there were many lilacs in full bloom. By one of those caprices that enter and give tinge to events without being at all a part of them, I find myself... reminded of the great tragedy of that day by the sight and odor of these blossoms.

The mortal voyage over, the ~~rocks~~ ~~and~~ ~~Tempests~~ + Tempests
pass'd gone the . . . once

The ship ~~it~~ ~~bears~~ me ~~safe~~ the . . . weight is won.

~~once comes home again~~ the ~~brave~~
~~an . . . bright — and~~ Close, . . . break
~~only slow is beaming;~~ . . .

The port is close, the bells ~~we~~ hear, the
As people all exulting,

While steady ~~comes~~ sails and enters straight the my
wondrous veteran vessel;

But O heart! heart! heart! ~~you~~ leave not
the little spot,

Where on the deck ~~my~~ Captain lies — sleeping
& dead. —

11.

O Captain! dearest captain! ~~wake~~ up yet
& hear the bells;

~~Wake~~ up & see the ~~shining~~ sun, & see the
~~flag a-flying;~~ . . .

For you it is the cities ~~want~~ about — for you the
shores are crowded;

For you the red-rose garlands, and the ~~loving~~ electric eyes
of women;

O captain! O my father! my arm I ~~place~~ push
~~around~~ beneath you;

It is some Dream that on the deck
you ~~lie~~ cold & dead.

An early draft of "O Captain! My Captain!," the most famous of Whitman's
poems inspired by the death of Abraham Lincoln.

260

[Abraham Lincoln] was assassinated—but the Union is not assassinated—... One falls, another falls. The soldier drops, sinks like a wave—but the ranks of the ocean eternally press on. Death does its work, obliterates a hundred, a thousand—President, general, captain, private—but the Nation is immortal.

261

The releas'd prisoners of war are now coming up from the southern prisons. I have seen a number of them. The sight is worse than any sight of battle-fields, or any collection of wounded, even the bloodiest. There was, (as a sample,) one large boat load, of several hundreds, brought about the 25th, to Annapolis; and out of the whole number only three individuals were able to walk from the boat. The rest were carried ashore and laid down in one place or another. Can those be *men*—those little livid brown, ash-streak'd, monkey-looking dwarfs?—are they really not mummied, dwindled corpses? They lay there, most of them, quite still, but with a horrible look in their eyes and skinny lips (often with not enough flesh on the lips to cover their teeth.)

MAY

262

When Sherman's armies, (long after they left Atlanta,) were marching through South and North Carolina—after leaving Savannah, the news of Lee's capitulation having been receiv'd—the men never mov'd a mile without from some part of the line sending up continued, inspiriting shouts. At intervals all day long sounded out the wild music of those peculiar army cries. They would be commenc'd by one regiment or brigade, immediately taken up by others, and at length whole corps and armies would join in these wild triumphant choruses. It was one of the characteristic expressions of the western troops, and became a habit, serving as a relief and outlet to the men—a vent for their feelings of victory, returning peace, &c. Morning, noon, and afternoon, spontaneous, for occasion or without occasion, these huge, strange cries, differing from any other, echoing through the open air for many a mile, expressing youth, joy, wildness, irrepressible strength, and the ideas of advance and conquest, sounded along the swamps and uplands of the South, floating to the skies. ('There never were men that kept in better spirits in danger or defeat—what then could they do in victory?'—said one of the 15th corps to me, afterwards.) This exuberance continued till the armies arrived at Raleigh. There the news of the President's murder was receiv'd.

263

[letter to a bereaved mother]

Dear madam: No doubt you and Frank's friends have heard the sad fact of his death in hospital here, through his uncle, or the lady from Baltimore, who took his things. (I have not seen them, only heard of them visiting Frank.) I will write you a few lines—as a casual friend that sat by his death-bed. Your son, corporal Frank H. Irwin, was wounded near fort Fisher, Virginia, March 25, 1865—the wound was in the left knee, pretty bad. He was sent up to Washington, was receiv'd in ward C, Armory-square hospital, March 28th—the wound became worse, and on the 4th of April the leg was amputated a little above the knee—the operation was perform'd by Dr. Bliss, one of the best surgeons in the army—he did the whole operation himself—there was a good deal of bad matter gather'd—the bullet was found in the knee. For a couple of weeks afterwards he was doing pretty well. I visited and sat by him frequently, as he was fond of having me. The last ten or twelve days of April I saw that his case was critical. He previously had some fever, with cold spells. The last week in April he was much of the time flighty—but always mild and gentle. He died first of May. The actual cause of death was pyaemia, (the absorption of the matter in the system instead of its discharge.)

Frank, as far as I saw, had everything requisite in surgical treatment, nursing, &c. He had watches much of the time. He was so good and well-behaved and affectionate, I myself liked him very much. I was in the habit of coming in afternoons and sitting by him, and soothing him, and he liked to have me—liked to put his arm out and lay his hand on my knee—would keep it so a long while. Toward the last he was more restless and flighty at night—often fancied himself with his regiment—by his talk sometimes seem'd as if his feelings were hurt by being blamed by his officers for something he was entirely innocent of—said, "I never in my life was thought capable of such a thing, and never was." At other times he would fancy himself talking as it seem'd to children or such like, his relatives I suppose, and giving them good advice; would talk to them a long while. All the time he was out of head not one single bad word or idea escaped him. It was remark'd that many a man's conversation in his senses was not half as good as Frank's delirium. He seem'd quite willing to die—he had become very weak and had suffer'd a good deal, and was perfectly resign'd, poor boy. I do not know his past life, but I feel as if it must have been good. At any rate what I saw of him here, under the most trying circumstances, with a painful wound; and among strangers, I can say that he behaved so brave, so composed, and so sweet and affectionate, it could not be surpass'd. And now like many other noble and good men, after serving his country as a soldier, he has yielded up his young life at the very outset in her service. Such things are gloomy—yet there is a text, "God doeth all things well"— the meaning of which, after due time, appears to the soul.

I thought perhaps a few words, though from a stranger, about your son, from one who was with him at the last, might be worth while—for I loved the young man, though I but saw him immediately to lose him. I am merely a friend visiting the hospitals occasionally to cheer the wounded and sick.

W. W.

May 21.—Saw General Sheridan and his cavalry to-day; a strong, attractive sight; the men were mostly young, (a few middle-aged,) superb-looking fellows, brown, spare, keen, with well-worn clothing, many with pieces of water-proof cloth around their shoulders, hanging down. They dash'd along pretty fast, in wide close ranks, all spatter'd with mud; no holiday soldiers; brigade after brigade. I could have watch'd for a week. Sheridan stood on a balcony, under a big tree, coolly smoking a cigar. His looks and manner impress'd me favorably....

May 22.—Have been taking a walk along Pennsylvania avenue and Seventh street north. The city is full of soldiers, running around loose. Officers everywhere, of all grades. All have the weather-beaten look of practical service. It is a sight I never tire of. All the armies are now here (or portions of them,) for to-morrow's review. You see them swarming like bees everywhere.

Well, the Review is over, & it was very grand—it was too much & too impressive, to be described—but [there will be] a good deal about it in the papers. If you can imagine a great wide avenue... quite flat, & stretching as far as you can see... & then through this avenue marching solid ranks of soldiers, 20 or 25 abreast, just marching steady all day long for two days, without intermission, one regiment after another, real war-worn *soldiers*, that have been marching & fighting for years—sometimes for an hour nothing but cavalry, just solid ranks, on good horses, with sabres glistening, & carbines hanging by their saddles, & their clothes showing hard service... —then great masses of guns, batteries of cannon, four or six abreast, each drawn by six horses, with the gunners seated on the ammunition wagons—& these perhaps a long while in passing, nothing but batteries—(it seemed as if all the cannon in the world were here)—then great battalions of blacks, with axes & shovels & pick axes, (real southern darkies, black as tar)—then again hour after hour the old infantry regiments, the men all sunburnt—nearly every one with some old tatter all in shreds, (that *had been* a costly & beautiful *flag*)—the great drum corps of sixty or eighty drummers massed at the heads of the brigades, playing away—now and then a fine brass band—but oftener nothing but the drums & whistling fifes—but they sounded very lively—(perhaps a band of sixty drums & fifteen or twenty fifes playing "Lannigan's ball")—the different corps banners, the generals with their staffs &c—the Western Army, led by Gen. Sherman, (old Bill, the soldiers call him)—... I saw the President several times, stood close by him, & took a good look at him—& like his expression much—he is very plain & substantial—it seemed wonderful that just that plain middling-sized ordinary man, dressed in black, without the least badge or ornament, should be the master of all these myriads of soldiers, the best that ever trod the earth, with forty or fifty Major-Generals, around him or riding by, with their broad yellow-satin belts around their waists—... I saw Gen. Grant too several times—He is the noblest Roman of them all—none of the pictures do justice to him—about sundown I saw him again riding on a large fine horse, with his hat off in answer to the hurrahs—he rode by where I stood, & I saw him well, as he rode by on a slow canter, with nothing but a single orderly after him—He looks like a good man—(& I believe there is much in looks)—I saw Gen. Meade, Gen. Thomas, Secretary Stanton, & lots of other celebrated government officers & generals—but the *rank & file* was the greatest sight of all.

266

May 28.—As I sat by the bedside of a sick Michigan soldier in hospital to-day, a convalescent from the adjoining bed rose and came to me, and presently we began talking. He was a middle-aged man, belonged to the 2d Virginia regiment, but lived in Racine, Ohio, and had a family there. He spoke of President Lincoln, and said: "The war is over, and many are lost. And now we have lost the best, the fairest, the truest man in America. Take him altogether, he was the best man this country ever produced. It was quite a while I thought very different; but some time before the murder, that's the way I have

seen it." There was deep earnestness in the soldier. (I found upon further talk he had known Mr. Lincoln personally, and quite closely,
years before.) He was a veteran; was now in the fifth year of his service; was a cavalry man, and had been in a good deal of hard fighting.

267

May 28-9.—I staid to-night a long time by the bedside of a new
patient, a young Baltimorean, aged about 19 years, W. S. P., (2d
Maryland, southern,) very feeble, right leg amputated, can't sleep
hardly at all—has taken a great deal of morphine, which, as usual, is
costing more than it comes to. Evidently very intelligent and well
bred—very affectionate—held on to my hand, and put it by his face,
not willing to let me leave. As I was lingering, soothing him in his
pain, he says to me suddenly, "I hardly think you know who I am—
I don't wish to impose upon you—I am a rebel soldier." I said I did
not know that, but it made no difference. Visiting him daily for
about two weeks after that, while he lived, (death had mark'd him,
and he was quite alone,) I loved him much, always kiss'd him, and he
did me. In an adjoining ward I found his brother, an officer of rank,
a Union soldier, a brave and religious man, (Col. Clifton K. Prentiss,
sixth Maryland infantry, Sixth corps, wounded in one of the engagements at Petersburgh, April 2—linger'd, suffer'd much, died.... It
was in the same battle both were hit.

268

James H. Williams, aged 21, 3d Virginia cavalry.—About as mark'd a
case of a strong man brought low by a complication of diseases,
(laryngitis, fever, debility and diarrhoea,) as I have ever seen—has
superb physique, remains swarthy yet, and flushed and red with
fever—is altogether flighty—flesh of his great breast and arms
tremulous, and pulse pounding away with treble quickness—lies a
good deal of the time in a partial sleep, but with low muttering and
groans—a sleep in which there is no rest. Powerful as he is, and so
young, he will not be able to stand many more days of the strain and
sapping heat of yesterday and to-day. His throat is in a bad way,

tongue and lips parch'd. When I ask him how he feels, he is able just to articulate, "I feel pretty bad yet, old man," and looks at me with his great bright eyes. Father, John Williams, Millensport, Ohio.

269

I buy, during the hot weather, boxes of oranges from time to time, and distribute them among the men; also preserved peaches and other fruits. Also lemons and sugar, for lemonade. Tobacco is also much in demand.

JUNE

270

Pennsylvania avenue looks unusually fine to-day. Of course it has not the character of Broadway, nor even... Fulton street, but it has a style of its own. Shoulder-straps, the crowds at hotels, strings of army wagons, the frequent patrols, &c., contribute their elements.

Passing down Pennsylvania avenue and entering the Capitol grounds, the first thing that strikes one is *the Flag*, beautiful and spiritual, up aloft there, out of the darkness, floating lovely as a dream, translucent the red stripes, with the spangled blue and white stars illuminated, delicate, very singular and clear, while all below is a mass of shade. Our Flag looks well anywhere, but it is never seen to more advantage than beaming there in the darkness, as if emanating its own light above the great dusky outlines of the architecture of the Capitol.

271

June 9-10.—I have been sitting late to-night by the bedside of a wounded captain, a special friend of mine, lying with a painful fracture of left leg in one of the hospitals, in a large ward partially vacant. The lights were put out, all but a little candle, far from where I sat.

Washington
June 10. 1865.

Mr. & Mrs. Pratt;

As I am visiting
your son Alfred occasionally, to cheer
him up in his sickness in hospital,
I thought you might like a few
words, though from a stranger, yet a
friend to your boy. I was there
last night, and sat a while by the
bed, as usual, & he showed me the
letter he had just received from home.
He wrote to you yesterday. He has
had diarrhea pretty bad, but is
now improved & goes about the
hospital — but as the weather is pretty
hot & powerful in the midst of the
day, I advised him not to go out
doors much at present. What he wants
most is rest, and a chance to get
his strength again. I expect he will

We are having very hot weather here, & it is Dry & dusty— The City is alive with soldiers from both the Army of the Potomac & the Western Armies, brought here by Sherman. There have been some great Reviews here, as you have seen in the papers — & thousands of soldiers are go' home every day.

You must write to Alfred often, as it cheers up a boy sick & away from home. Write all about Domestic & farm incidents, and as cheerful as may be. Direct to him, in Ward C. Armory Square Hospital, Washington, D.C. Should any thing occur, I will write you again, but I feel confident he will continue doing well. For the present farewell.

Walt Whitman
Washington
D C

The full moon shone in through the windows, making long, slanting silvery patches on the floor. All was still, my friend too was silent, but could not sleep; so I sat there by him, slowing wafting the fan, and occupied with the musings that arose out of the scene, the long shadowy ward, the beautiful ghostly moonlight on the floor, the white beds, here and there an occupant with huddled form, the bed-clothes thrown off. The hospitals have a number of cases of sun-stroke and exhaustion by heat, from the late reviews.

JULY

272

The grounds on [the back or west side of the Capitol] are not large, but kept in perfection. I go there occasionally of an afternoon. The dense shade is a great help. The trees are plenty, some of them large, some of them giving out aromatic smells. I find there, (I think the light is extra-powerful here,) besides a large effect of green, varied with the white of the Capitol, fountains playing, locusts whirring, the grass-cutters whetting their scythes, the chirp of robins, the tinkling of the Georgetown and Navy-yard cars as they wind the hill, a few lazy promenaders, soldiers, some with crutches or one-armed, come to take a look, and lots of loungers on the iron settees, completely sheltered from the sun by the dense umbrage.

273

It is Sunday afternoon, middle of summer, hot and oppressive, and very silent through the ward. I am taking care of a critical case, now lying in a half lethargy.

274

The war is over, but the hospitals are fuller than ever, from former and current cases. A large majority of the wounds are in the arms and legs. But there is every kind of wound, in every part of the body. I should say of the sick, from my observation, that the prevailing maladies are typhoid fever and the camp fevers generally, diarrhoea, catarrhal affections and bronchitis, rheumatism and pneumonia. These forms of sickness lead; all the rest follow. There are twice as many sick as there are wounded. The deaths range from seven to ten per cent. of those under treatment.

275

Harlowe was only 22 years of age—was a tall, slim, dark-hair'd, blue-eyed young man—had come out originally with the 29th [Massachusetts]…. He was in the Seven Days fight before Richmond, in second Bull Run, Antietam, first Fredericksburgh, Vicksburgh, Jackson, Wilderness, and the campaigns following—was as good a soldier as ever wore the blue, and every old officer in the regiment will bear that testimony. Though so young, and in a common rank, he had a spirit as resolute and brave as any hero in the books, ancient or modern— It was too great to say the words "I surrender"— and so he died. (When I think of such things, knowing them well, all the vast and complicated events of the war, on which history dwells and makes its volumes, fall aside, and for the moment at any rate I see nothing but young Calvin Harlowe's figure in the night, disdaining to surrender.)

276

…George W. Whitman—in active service all through, four years, re-enlisting twice—was promoted, step by step, (several times immediately after battles,) lieutenant, captain, major and lieut. colonel—was in the actions at Roanoke, Newbern, 2d Bull Run, Chantilly, South Mountain, Antietam, Fredericksburgh, Vicksburgh, Jackson, the bloody conflicts of the Wilderness, and at Spottsylvania, Cold Harbor, and afterwards around Petersburgh; at one of these latter was taken prisoner, and pass'd four or five months in secesh military prisons, narrowly escaping with life, from a severe fever, from starvation and half-nakedness in the winter. (What a history that 51st New York had! Went out early—march'd, fought everywhere—was in storms at sea, nearly wreck'd—storm'd forts—tramp'd hither and yon in Virginia, night and day, summer of '62—afterwards Kentucky and Mississippi—re-enlisted—was in all the engagements and campaigns, as above.) I strengthen and comfort myself much with the certainty that the capacity for just such regiments, (hundreds, thousands of them) is inexhaustible in the United States....

AUGUST

277

Tuesday, Aug. 1, 1865.—About 3 o'clock this afternoon (sun broiling hot) in Fifteenth street, by the Treasury building, a large and handsome regiment, 195th Pennsylvania, were marching by—as it happen'd, receiv'd orders just here to halt and break ranks, so that they might rest themselves awhile. I thought I never saw a finer set of men—so hardy, candid, bright American looks, all weather-beaten, and with [worn?] clothes. Every man was home-born. My heart was much drawn toward them. They seem'd very tired, red, and streaming with sweat. It is a one-year regiment, mostly from Lancaster County, Pa; have been in Shenandoah Valley. On halting, the men unhitch'd their knapsacks, and sat down to rest themselves. Some lay flat on the pavement or under trees. The fine physical appearance of the whole body was remarkable. Great, very great, must be the State where such young farmers and mechanics are in the practical average. I went around for half an hour and talk'd with several of them, sometimes squatting down with the groups.

278

There was a big match played here yesterday between two base ball clubs, one from Philadelphia & the other a Washington club—& today another is to come off between a New York & the Philadelphia club I believe—thousands go to see them play—
I keep well, & every body says I am getting fat & hearty—

I am working now in the Attorney General's office. This is the place where the big southerners now come up to get pardoned—all the rich men & big officers of the reb army have to get special pardons.... There are between 4 & 5000 pardons issued from this Office, but only about 200 have been signed by the President—The rest he is letting wait, till he gets good & ready—What I hear & see about Andrew Johnson, I think he is a *good man*—sometimes some of the letters he gets are sent over to this office to be answered—& occasionally that job falls to me—One of them was a letter a few days ago from a widow woman in Westfield, N Y. Her husband was in Texas when the war broke out, joined *our* army—& was killed by the rebels—they also confiscated his property in Texas, leaving his family helpless—this lady wrote to the President for aid, &c.—I wrote the President's answer—telling her that she should have her husband's pension, which would be pretty good, as he was a captain—& that the rebs in Texas could not hold any such property, but that she could bring a suit & get it back, &c.—then put in a few words to cheer her up, &c.—

280

Attorney General's Office, Washington, Aug. 22, 1865—As I write this, about noon, the suite of rooms here is fill'd with southerners, standing in squads, or streaming in and out, some talking with the Pardon Clerk, some waiting to see the Attorney General, others discussing in low tones among themselves. All are mainly anxious about their pardons. The famous 13th exception of the President's Amnesty Proclamation of ——, makes it necessary that every secessionist, whose property is worth $20,000 or over, shall get a special pardon, before he can transact any legal purchase, sale, &c. So hundreds and thousands of such property owners have either sent up here, for the last two months, or have been, or are now coming personally here, to get their pardons. They are from Virginia, Georgia, Alabama, Mississippi, North and South Carolina, and every southern State. Some of their written petitions are very abject. Secession officers of the rank of Brigadier General, or higher, also need these special pardons. They also come here. I see streams of the $20,000 men, (and some women,) every day. I talk now and then with them, and learn much that is interesting and significant. All the southern women that come (some splendid specimens, mothers, &c.) are dress'd in deep black....

The crowds that come here make a curious study for me. I get along, very sociably, with any of them—as I let them do all the talking; only now and then I have a long confab, or ask a suggestive question or two.

If the thing continues as at present, the property and wealth of the Southern States is going to legally rest, for the future, on these pardons. Every single one is made out with the condition that the grantee shall respect the abolition of slavery, and never make an attempt to restore it.

SEPTEMBER

281

Sep. 10.—Visited Douglas and Stanton hospitals. They are quite full. Many of the cases are bad ones, lingering wounds, and old sickness. There is a more than usual look of despair on the countenances of many of the men; hope has left them. I went through the wards, talking as usual. There are several here from the confederate army whom I had seen in other hospitals, and they recognized me. Two were in a dying condition.

282

September 22, '65.—Afternoon and evening at Douglas Hospital to see a friend belonging to 2d New York Artillery (Hiram W. Frazee, Serg't,) down with an obstinate compound fracture of left leg receiv'd in one of the last battles near Petersburg. After sitting a while with him, went through several neighboring wards. In one of them found an old acquaintance transferr'd here lately, a rebel prisoner, in a dying condition. Poor fellow, the look was already on his face. He gazed long at me. I ask'd him if he knew me. After a moment he utter'd something, but inarticulately. I have seen him off and on for the last five months. He has suffer'd very much; a bad wound in left leg, severely fractured, several operations, cuttings, extractions of bone, splinters, &c. I remember he seem'd to me, as I used to talk with him, a fair specimen of the main strata of the Southerners, those without property or education, but still with the stamp which comes from freedom and equality. I liked him; Jonathan Wallace, of Hurd Co., Georgia, age 30 (wife, Susan F. Wallace, Houston, Hurd Co., Georgia.) Had a family; had not heard from them since taken prisoner, now six months. I had written for him, and done trifles for him, before he came here. He made no outward show, was mild in his talk and behavior, but I knew he worried much inwardly. But now all would be over very soon. I half sat upon the little stand near the head of the bed. Wallace was somewhat restless. I placed my hand lightly on his forehead and face, just sliding it over the surface. In a moment or so he fell into a calm, regular-breathing lethargy or sleep, and remain'd so while I sat there. It was dark, and the lights were lit. I hardly know why (death seem'd hovering near,) but I stay'd nearly an hour. A Sister of Charity, dress'd in black, with a broad white linen bandage around her head and under her chin, and a black crape over all and flowing down from her head in long wide pieces, came to him, and moved around the bed. She bow'd low and solemn to me.

OCTOBER

283

October 3.—There are two army hospitals now remaining. I went to the largest of these (Douglas) and spent the afternoon and evening. There are many sad cases, old wounds, incurable sickness, and some of the wounded from the March and April battles before Richmond. Few realize how sharp and bloody these closing battles were. Our

WE, the Subscribers, acknowledge to have received from *S. M. McKean Esq.*, Disbursing Clerk, Treasury Dep't, the sums opposite our respective names, in full of our salaries in the *Attorney General's Office* for *October*, 1865.

NAMES.	CAPACITY.	AMOUNT. Annual Salary.	AMOUNT. Month. Dollars	AMOUNT. Month. Cents	AMOUNT TAXABLE.	AMOUNT OF TAX. 5 per cent.	NET AMOUNT.	SIGNATURES.
James Speed	Atty. Genl.	8000	673	91	623 37	31 17	642 74	James Speed
J. Hubley Ashton	Asst. Atty Gen.	3500	294	84	244 29	12 21	282 63	J Hubley Ashton
Wm. Stewart	Chief Clk.	2200	185	33	134 78	6 74	178 59	Wm Stewart
M. F. Pleasants	Pard. Clk.	1800	151	63	101 09	5 05	146 58	M. F. Pleasants
J. A. Rowland	Opin. Clk.	1800	151	63	101 09	5 05	146 58	J A Rowland
F. W. Stitt	3. Class Clk.	1600	134	78	84 24	4 21	130 57	F W Stitt
A. L. Kerr	3. Class Clk.	1600	134	78	84 24	4 21	130 57	A L Kerr
Hugh Rowland	1. Class Clk.	1200	101	09	50 55	2 53	98 56	Hugh Rowland
Walt. Whitman	Temp. Clk.	1200	101	09	50 55	2 53	98 56	Walt. Whitman
Louis R. McLain	Temp. Clk.	1200	101	09	50 55	2 53	98 56	Louis R. McLain
H. A. Klopfer	Messenger	1000	84	24	33 70	1 69	82 55	Henry A. Klopfer
			2114	41			2036 49	

*Attorney General's Office payroll sheet
showing Whitman's pay as "temporary clerk."*

men exposed themselves more than usual; press'd ahead without urging. Then the southerners fought with extra desperation. Both sides knew that with the successful chasing of the rebel cabal from Richmond, and the occupation of that city by the national troops, the game was up. The dead and wounded were unusually many. Of the wounded the last lingering driblets have been brought to hospital here. I find many rebel wounded here, and have been extra busy today 'tending to the worst cases of them with the rest.

284

As I turn'd off the Avenue one cool October evening into Thirteenth street, a soldier with knapsack and overcoat stood at the corner inquiring his way. I found he wanted to go part of the road in my direction, so we walk'd on together. We soon fell into conversation. He was small and not very young, and a tough little fellow, as I judged in the evening light, catching glimpses by the lamps we pass'd. His answers were short, but clear. His name was Charles Carroll; he belong'd to one of the Massachusetts regiments, and was born in or near Lynn. His parents were living, but were very old. There were four sons, and all had enlisted. Two had died of starvation and misery in the prison at Andersonville, and one had been kill'd in the west. He only was left. He was now going home, and by the way he talk'd I inferr'd that his time was nearly out. He made great calculations on being with his parents to comfort them the rest of their days.

NOVEMBER

285

A great recreation, the past three years, has been in taking long walks out from Washington, five, seven, perhaps ten miles and back... over the perfect military roads, hard and smooth—... The roads connecting Washington and the numerous forts around the city, made one useful result, at any rate, out of the war.

DECEMBER

286

The only remaining hospital is now "Harewood," out in the woods, northwest of the city. I have been visiting there regularly every Sunday, during [the past] two months.

287

Dec. 10—Sunday.—Again spending a good part of the day at Harewood. I write this about an hour before sundown. I have walk'd out for a few minutes to the edge of the woods to soothe myself with the hour and scene. It is a glorious, warm, golden-sunny, still afternoon. The only noise is from a crowd of cawing crows, on some trees three hundred yards distant. Clusters of gnats swimming and dancing in the air in all directions. The oak leaves are thick under the bare trees, and give a strong and delicious perfume. Inside the wards everything is gloomy. Death is there. As I enter'd, I was confronted by it the first thing; a corpse of a poor soldier, just dead of typhoid fever. The attendants had just straighten'd the limbs, put coppers on the eyes, and were laying it out.

288

I have at night watched by the side of a sick man in the hospital, one who could not live many hours. I have seen his eyes flash and burn as he raised himself and recurr'd to the cruelties on his surrender'd brother, and mutilations of the corpse afterward. (See, in the preceding pages, the incident at Upperville—the seventeen kill'd as in the description, were left there on the ground. After they dropt dead, no one touch'd them—all were made sure of, however. The carcasses were left for the citizens to bury or not, as they chose.) Such was the war. It was not a quadrille in a ball-room.

Final Year of Service, 1866

"The dome-crown'd capitol there on the hill, so stately over the trees..."

JANUARY 24, '66.—Went out to Harewood early to-day, and remain'd all day.

Sunday, February 4, 1866.—Harewood Hospital again. Walk'd out this afternoon (bright, dry, ground frozen hard) through the woods. Ward 6 is fill'd with blacks, some with wounds, some ill, two or three with limbs frozen. The boys made quite a picture sitting round the stove. Hardly any can read or write. I write for three or four, direct envelopes, give some tobacco, &c.

Joseph Winder, a likely boy, aged twenty-three, belongs to 10th Color'd Infantry (now in Texas;) is from Eastville, Virginia. Was a slave; belong'd to Lafayette Homeston. The master was quite willing he should leave. Join'd the army two years ago; has been in one or two battles. Was sent to the hospital with rheumatism. Has since been employ'd as cook. His parents at Eastville; he gets letters from them, and has letters written to them by a friend. Many black boys left that part of Virginia and join'd the army; the 10th, in fact, was made up of Virginia blacks from thereabouts. As soon as discharged is going back to Eastville to his parents and home, and intends to stay there.

Thomas King, formerly 2d District Color'd Regiment, discharged soldier, Company E, lay in a dying condition; his disease was consumption. A Catholic priest was administering extreme unction to him. (I have seen this kind of sight several times in the hospitals; it is very impressive.)

291

Harewood, April 29, 1866.—Sunday afternoon.—Poor Joseph Swiers, Company H, 155th Pennsylvania, a mere lad (only eighteen years of age;) his folks living in Reedsburg, Pennsylvania. I have known him now for nearly a year, transferr'd from hospital to hospital. He was badly wounded in the thigh at Hatcher's Run, February 6, '65.

James E. Ragan, Atlanta, Georgia; 2d United States Infantry. Union folks. Brother impress'd, deserted, died; now no folks, left alone in the world, is in a singularly nervous state; came in hospital with intermittent fever.

Walk slowly around the ward, observing, and to see if I can do anything.

292

During [these last] three years in hospital, camp or field, I [have] made over six hundred visits or tours, and [gone], as I estimate, counting all, among from eighty thousand to a hundred thousand of the wounded and sick, as sustainer of spirit and body in some degree, in time of need. These visits varied from an hour or two, to all day or night; for with dear or critical cases I generally watch'd all night. Sometimes I took up my quarters in the hospital, and slept or watch'd there several nights in succession. Those three years I consider the greatest privilege and satisfaction, (with all their feverish excitements and physical deprivations and lamentable sights,) and, of course, the most profound lesson of my life. I can say that in my ministerings I comprehended all, whoever came in my way, northern or southern, and slighted none.

293

Before I went down to the Field, and among the Hospitals, I had my hours of doubt about These States; but not since. The bulk of the Army, to me, develop'd, transcended, in personal qualities—and, radically, in moral ones—all that the most enthusiastic Democratic-

Republican ever fancied, idealized in loftiest dreams. And curious as it may seem, the War, to me, *proved* Humanity, and proved America and the Modern.

(I think I am perfectly well aware of the corruption and wickedness of my lands and days—the general political, business and social shams and shysterisms, everywhere. Heaven knows, I see enough of them—running foul of them continually! But I also see the noblest elements in society—and not in specimens only, but vast, enduring, inexhaustible strata of them—ruggedness, simplicity, courage, love, wit, health, liberty, patriotism—all the virtues, the main bulk, public and private.)

Walt Whitman in 1869, three years after finishing his service in the military hospitals.

SOURCES AND ACKNOWLEDGMENTS

This appendix gives the sources of the 293 numbered entries in *The Sacrificial Years*. The abbreviations used in listing the sources are:

Cor   *The Collected Writings of Walt Whitman. The Correspondence, Vol. I: 1842-1867.* Ed. Edwin Haviland Miller. New York: New York University Press, 1961.

DBed   *The Works of Walt Whitman in Two Volumes, As Prepared By Him For the Deathbed Edition. Vol. II, The Collected Prose.* New York: Minerva Press, 1969. (A reprint of the text of Whitman's collected works published just before his death in 1892.)

CW   *Walt Whitman and the Civil War: A Collection of Original Articles and Manuscripts.* Ed. Charles I. Glicksburg. Philadelphia: University of Pennsylvania Press, 1933.

FC   *Faint Clews & Indirections: Manuscripts of Walt Whitman and His Family.* Ed. Clarence Gohdes and Rollo G. Silver. Durham, N.C.: Duke University Press, 1949.

MSN   Civil War manuscript notebooks of Walt Whitman in the Library of Congress, Manuscript Division, Thomas Biggs Harned Walt Whitman Collection.

SD   *The Collected Writings of Walt Whitman. Prose Works 1892: Vol. I, Specimen Days.* Ed. Floyd Stovall. New York: New York University Press, 1963.

SS   Gay Wilson Allen. *The Solitary Singer: A Critical Biography of Walt Whitman.* New York: New York University Press, 1967.

UPP *The Uncollected Poetry and Prose of Walt Whitman*. Vol. II, Ed. Emory Holloway. New York: Peter Smith, 1932.

WD Walt Whitman, *The Wound Dresser: A Series of Letters Written from the Hospitals in Washington During the War of the Rebellion*. Ed. Richard Maurice Bucke, M.D. Boston: Small, Maynard & Company, 1898.

The numbers in bold face below refer to the corresponding entry in the text. Following the entry number is the relevant source abbreviation and page numbers. No page numbers are given for the seven entries from Whitman's manuscript notebooks in the Harned Collection.

1 SD 23-24; **2** SD 25-26; **3** SD 26-29; **4** SD 30-31; **5** CW 42-43; **6** CW 82; **7** WD 47-49; **8** CW 70-71; **9** CW 79; **10** CW 67; **11** MSN; **12** CW 69; **13** CW 71-72; **14** CW 70; **15** CW 70, SD 32, 33; **16** CW 69-70, 68-69; **17** CW 80-81; **18** CW 79; **19** CW 73, 74; **20** SD 34-35; **21** SD 296; **22** WD 53-54; **23** SD 50; **24** SD 51; **25** SD 51; **26** SD 51; **27** SD 43; **28** Cor 70; **29** MSN; **30** SD 43; **31** Cor 67; **32** SD 69; **33** MSN; **34** SD 100; **35** SD 304; **36** SD 308; **37** SD 298-299; **38** SD 38; **39** WD 58-59; **40** SD 319; **41** SD 40-41; **42** SD 39; **43** SD 39; **44** SD 318; **45** SD 39-40; **46** WD 59-60; **47** Cor 77; **48** SD 62-63; **49** Cor 76;

 50 CW 172; **51** Cor 79-80; **52** Cor 80; **53** Cor 81; **54** CW 163; **55** Cor 77-78; **56** Cor 81; **57** Cor 82-83; **58** Cor 83-84; **59** Cor 84-85; **60** WD 61; **61** Cor 92; **62** WD 66-67; **63** WD 64-65; **64** SD 67-68; **65** WD 67; **66** WD 70; **67** CW 133-134; **68** SD 44; **69** Cor 98; **70** WD 75; **71** WD 73-74; **72** SD 46; **73** WD 74; **74** Cor 102; **75** SD 51-52; **76** WD 76-77; **77** SD 52-53; **78** SD 64; **79** SD 51; **80** WD 79; **81** Cor 99; **82** SD 318; **83** WD 83; **84** WD 82; **85** WD 84-85; **86** SD 49-50; **87** WD 86; **88** WD 85; **89** WD 86-87; **90** WD 89; **91** WD 87-89; **92** WD 90-92; **93** WD 92; **94** SD 53-54; **95** SD 54-55; **96** SD 55; **97** WD 93-94; **98** WD 96; **99** SD 56-57;

 100 Cor 119; **101** Cor 122; **102** Cor 127, 129-130; **103** Cor 122-123; **104** SD 57-59; **105** SD 59-61; **106** WD 101-102; **107** Cor 123-124; **108** WD 99; **109** WD 97-98; **110** DBed 462; **111** Cor 142; **112** WD 107;

113 MSN; 114 WD 113; 115 Cor 142; 116 WD 114-115; 117 SD 68; 118 SD 65-67; 119 WD 120; 120 WD 111-112; 121 MSN; 122 WD 108; 123 WD 118-119; 124 WD 106-107; 125 WD 130-131; 126 DBed 461; 127 UPP 31-33; 128 WD 123-124; 129 CW 162-163; 130 WD 127; 131 UPP 33-34; 132 Cor 154; 133 Cor 155; 134 Cor 155; 135 Cor 154; 136 Cor 154; 137 Cor 168; 138 Cor 159-160; 139 WD 136-137; 140 SD 67; 141 WD 138-139; 142 WD 128-129; 143 SD 83-84; 144 Cor 176, 178-179; 145 Cor 180; 146 Cor 181; 147 Cor 185; 148 Cor 182; 149 Cor 185;

150 Cor 188; 151 WD 145; 152 SD 74-75; 153 SD 76-77; 154 SD 79-81; 155 WD 146-147; 156 DBed 434; 157 Cor 196; 158 SD 71-72; 159 SD 70; 160 WD 151; 161 SD 69-70; 162 WD 149-150; 163 WD 150-151; 164 SD 70-71; 165 WD 149; 166 FC 70-71; 167 SD 72; 168 SD 79; 169 UPP 28; 170 WD 153; 171 Cor 202; 172 WD 154-155; 173 WD 156; 174 UPP 28; 175 WD 158; 176 WD 158-159; 177 WD 160; 178 WD 162; 179 DBed 432-433; 180 WD 163-164; 181 WD 164; 182 WD 165; 183 WD 166-168; 184 DBed 435; 185 WD 168-169; 186 WD 170-171; 187 Cor 215; 188 SD 81-82; 189 SD 73-74; 190 WD 177; 191 WD 178; 192 WD 180-181; 193 DBed 463; 194 WD 187; 195 Cor 226; 196 DBed 463-464; 197 UPP 36, 27; 198 Cor 227; 199 SD 75;

200 WD 190-191; 201 Cor 230; 202 WD 192-195; 203 WD 196; 204 WD 197; 205 Cor 234; 206 Cor 237; 207 Cor 235-236; 208 Cor 239; 209 MSN; 210 CW 164-165; 211 MSN; 212 SD 307; 213 CW 159; 214 Cor 241-242; 215 Cor 242; 216 Cor 240; 217 Cor 243; 218 Cor 243; 219 UPP 40; 220 SD 307; 221 Cor 244; 222 SS 318-319; 223 CW 178-180; 224 Cor 246-247; 225 Cor 247; 226 SD 91-92; 227 SD 86-87; 228 DBed 464-465; 229 DBed 465-466; 230 DBed 465; 231 Cor 250; 232 SS 323; 233 Cor 253; 234 Cor 254; 235 SD 78-79; 236 SD 309; 237 SD 306; 238 SS 326; 239 Cor 255; 240 SD 85; 241 SD 321; 242 SD 93; 243 SD 91; 244 SD 317; 245 SD 95; 246 SD 95-96; 247 UPP 30-31; 248 SD 92; 249 SD 83;

250 SD 87-88; 251 SD 88; 252 Cor 256-257; 253 Cor 257; 254 CW 174; 255 CW 174-175; 256 SD 31; 257 DBed 316-317; 258 SD 94-95; 259 SS 355; 260 SD 99; 261 SD 100-101; 262 SD 99; 263 SD 103-104; 264 SD 105; 265 Cor 260-262; 266 SD 106-107; 267 SD 106; 268 SD 108; 269 SD 303; 270 UPP 27, 43; 271 SD 108; 272 SD 301; 273 SD 76; 274 SD 97-98; 275 SD 97; 276 SD 111-112; 277 DBed 433; 278 Cor 266;

279 Cor 265; **280** DBed 456; **281** SD 108-109; **282** DBed 466-467; **283** SD 109-110; **284** SD 77; **285** SD 111; **286** DBed 467; **287** SD 110; **288** SD 116-117; **289** DBed 467; **290** DBed 467; **291** DBed 467-468; **292** SD 113; **293** SD 323.

Entries from *The Correspondence, Vol. I: 1842-1867, Specimen Days,* and *The Solitary Singer* (abbreviated above Cor, SD, and SS) are reprinted by the kind permission of New York University Press; entry 166 (from *Faint Clews & Indirections*) is reprinted with the permission of Duke University Press; and entries 11, 29, 33, 113, 121, 209, and 211 are reprinted courtesy of the Library of Congress, Manuscript Division, Thomas Biggs Harned Walt Whitman Collection.

The photographs of Walt Whitman, George Whitman, Whitman's soldier friends, the anonymous amputee, the 110th Pennsylvania Infantry, the manuscripts of Whitman's poem and letter, his annotated photo of Lincoln, and his Christian Commission certificate are from the Charles E. Feinberg Collection, Library of Congress. The photographs of Abraham Lincoln, Fredericksburg in ruins, Trinity Church, Christian Commission headquarters, Brandy Station in 1863, the dead Union soldier, the dead Confederate soldier, the field hospital, the tent hospital, the farmhouse hospital, the four-wheeled ambulances, the shelters at Antietam, the 9th Corps hospital stewards, the Finlay Hospital surgeons, the Armory Square, Campbell, Quartermaster's, and Stanton hospitals, and the ward in Harewood Hospital are from the Civil War collections of the Library of Congress. The photographs of the hospital at Savage Station, Antietam, the Chancellorsville wounded, and the completed Capitol; the portraits of Stanton, Sumner, Grant, and Lee; the engravings of Harewood Hospital, the Battle of Bull Run, the view of Washington with unfinished Capitol dome, and the "Letter for Home"; and the endpaper engravings of Douglas & Stanton Hospitals and Campbell Hospital are from the Boston Athenæum. The portrait of Lincoln, the "Hoosier Michael Angelo," is from the National Archives, Washington, D.C. The photograph of winter quarters at Brandy Station is from the U. S. Army Military History Institute, Carlisle, Pennsylvania. The photograph of the Attorney General's payroll is from the Walt Whitman House, Camden, New Jersey.

The publishers gratefully acknowledge the photographic research of Sally Pierce and Pamela Greiff of the Boston Athenæum and of Diane Hamilton, Washington, D.C.

INDEX

〰〰〰

Allen, Ashbury, 60

America. *See also* Genius of America (statue)

  foundation of, xvii, 35, 123–124, 132

  the genuine, 29, 61, 87, 154–155

Amnesty Proclamation, 144

Antietam, Battle of, 64, 122, 142

Aquia Creek, 17–18, 23

Armory Square Hospital, 17–18, 21, 39, 46, 49, 52, 55, 69, 72, 99, 101, 133

Army Hospital Volunteer, work of, 22

Army of the Potomac. *See* Potomac, Army of the

Army Paymaster's office, xv, 25, 34

Ashby, Gen. Turner, 83

Astor House, 127, 129

Attorney General's office, xv, 144

Babcock, Lt., 108

Ballooning, 12–13

Ball Plain, Battle of, 100

Barker, John, 61

Baseball, 143

Beeman, Willard, 104

Billings, Miss/Mrs., 125

Black soldiers, xvii, 48, 63, 93, 153

Bliss, Dr., 68

Books for soldiers, 94–95

Borley, Pleasant, 60

Broadway Hospital, 7

Brooklyn City Hospital, 104

Brooks, Livingston, 47

Bucke, Richard, xviii

Bull Run, Battle of, 4–6, 27

Bull Run, Second Battle of, 10, 72, 122, 142

Burnside, Gen. Ambrose, 92, 99

Byrd, Thomas, 108–109

Campbell, L.H., 24

Campbell Hospital, 19–20, 22, 62

Camp of Instruction, 9

Capitol Building, 28, 30, 63, 65–66, 92, 138, 141

Carroll, Charles, 148

Carver Hospital, 98–99

Central Park Hospital, 107

Chancellorsville, Battle of, 37–38, 41–42, 55

Chase, Secretary of the Treasury Salmon, 25–26, 33

Chauncey, Charles, 57–58

Christ, 13

Christian Commission, 46

Civil War

  European view of, 120–121

  lesson of, xvii

  news of outbreak received in New York City, 3

  proportion of combat casualties, xi–xii

  Walt Whitman's perspective on, xiv

Clay, Henry, 128

Clocum's Creek, 10

Combatants in Civil War, motives of, xii–xiii

Combat casualties, proportions in Civil War, xi–xii

Company A

  1st Regular Cavalry, 60

  9th U.S. Cavalry, 59

  78th New York, 46

  101st New York, 72

Company B

  17th Pennsylvania Cavalry, 47

  111th Pennsylvania, 60

Company D, 27th Indiana, 60

Company E

  1st Delaware, 20

  2nd District Colored Regiment, 153

  5th Wisconsin, 97

  51st New York Volunteers, 11

Company F
  2nd New Jersey Volunteers, 18
  2nd U.S. Cavalry, 60
  142nd New York, 21
Company G
  51st New York Volunteers, 10
  108th New York, 60
  154th New York, 51
Company H
  17th Connecticut, 25
  55th Ohio, 60
  155th Pennsylvania, 154
Company I, 35th Massachusetts, 19
Company J, 100th Pennsylvania, 20
Company K
  2nd Pennsylvania Volunteers, 104
  141st New York, 51, 53
Company M
  2nd New York Cavalry, 68
  4th New York Cavalry, 44
Comradship, xv
Congress, 30, 33, 91, 114, 122–123
Connecticut, New Canaan, 25
Cotrel, Thomas, 38
Cunningham, Oscar, 95, 98–99
Cutter, Charles, 96

Dante, 31
Death, confronting, xvi, 14, 48, 59, 132, 149
Delaware, Georgetown, 63, 141
Deserters, 87, 90
District of Columbia. See Washington, D.C.
Douglas Hospital, 145–146
Draft riots, 50, 57
Drum-Taps, 75, 88, 102, 113, 126

82nd Ohio, 95
83nd Pennsylvania, 104
11th New Hampshire volunteers, 14
Elliot, John, 39
Emerson, Ralph Waldo.
Emory Hospital, 32

Ferrero, Gen., 8–10, 92
5th Connecticut Volunteers, 21

5th Wisconsin, 97
51st New York Volunteers, xv, xviii, 9–14, 19, 105–107, 120, 142–143
Finley Hospital, 62
1st Delaware, 20
1st Massachusetts Heavy Artillery, 96
1st Pennsylvania Cavalry, 19
1st Regular Cavalry, 60
Food and drink for soldiers, 10–11, 40, 43, 98–99, 124–125, 138
Ford, Joshua, 20
Fort Fisher, 133
Fort Monroe, 68
Fort Sumter, attack on, xiv, 3
Francis, Capt., 8
Frazee, Hiram, 145
Fredericksburg, Battle of, xv, 19, 22–23, 38, 86, 100, 122, 142
Fulton ferry-boat, 4

Gardiner, Richard, 20
Genius of America (statue), 65–66
Georgia, Atlanta, 154
Gettysburg, Battle of, 49
Gilliland, Maj., 20
Glicksberg, Charles, xix
Glover, Stewart, 97–98
Grant, Gen. Ulysses, 88–89, 99, 117, 136
Gray, Fred, 105

Haley, Thomas, 44
Hancock, Gen. Winfield, 97
Hapgood, Maj., 54, 71, 86, 99, 101
Harewood Hospital, 149, 153–154
Harlowe, Calvin, 142
Harrington, by O'Connor, 43
Haskell, Erastus, 51–54, 70
Hatcher's Run, Battle of, 154
Health. See Physical health; Whitman, Walt
Hicks, Elias, 46
Hogan, Dr., 7
Holmes, John, 18, 47
Hooker, Gen. Joseph, 37–38, 40
Hospitals. See Military hospitals
Huse, Frederick, 19

Indiana
    Epton, 60
    Noblesville, 60
Indian Bureau office, xv, 117
Interior Department, 117
Irwin, Frank, 133–134

Jackson, Battle of, 142
Jackson, President Andrew, 128
Johnson, President Andrew, 144

Kilpatrick's Cavalry, 65
King, Preston, 25–26
King, Thomas, 153
Kossuth, Lajos, 128

Lacy House, 12, 32
Lafayette, Marquis de, 128
Leaves of Grass, xiii
Lee, Gen. Robert E., 46, 48–50, 73
LeGendre, Col., 95–96
Library of Congress, xviii
Lincoln, President Abraham, 6, 32–33, 49,
    56–57, 71, 94, 124
    character of, 6, 32–33, 49, 136–137
    death of, 126–133
    Whitman's recollection, 127–129
Lindly, Thomas, 19
Livenspargh, Isaac, 60
Logan, John, 104
Lowenfels, Walter, xix

Mack, Mrs., 7
Mahay, John, 72
Maine, East Livermore, 19
Maryland, Annapolis, 9
Massachusetts
    Campello, 18, 22–25
    Lawrence City, 96
    Lynn, 148
McClellan, Gen. George, 29, 105
Meade, Gen. George, 49–50, 65, 72, 82, 84,
    95, 136
Meigs, Gen. Montgomery, 26
"Memoranda," xviii
Metropolitan Hotel, 3

Michaelangelo, 33
Military hospitals, xv–xvii, 17, 43, 69, 85
    staff of, 21–22, 104, 125
    wounded Confederates in, xvii,
    114–116
Mitchelle, Henry, 21
Modernity, 155
Monk, George, 46
Moore, Amer, 42
Morgan, John, 116
Moseby, John Singleton, 79–80

Neat, Thomas, 70
Neuse River, 10
New York
    Batavia, 98
    Comac, 68
    Glen's Falls, 60
    Webster, 60
    Westfield, 144
    West Hills, xiv
New York Academy of Music, 73
New York City, 72–76, 105, 143
    Broadway, 127
    Brooklyn, xiv–xvi, 3–4, 10–11, 19, 54,
    70, 72, 74, 101–107, 126
    Canal Street, 127
    Coney Island, 105–106
    draft riots in, 50, 57
    Jamaica, 70
    news of war's outbreak received in, 3
New York newspapers, 6, 127
New York University Press, xix
9th U.S. Cavalry, 59
North Carolina
    Hatteras, 9–10
    Newbern, 10
    Raleigh, 133
    Salisbury, 118
    Shellot, 116
Northrup, D.L., 38
Northrup, Willis, 60
Notebooks, xviii

"O Captain! My Captain!", 126–132
O'Connor, Mr. and Mrs., 43

Odd Fellows Lodge, 49
Ohio
    Camp Chase, 116
    Lykenston, 60
    Millensport, 138
    Racine, 136
100th Pennsylvania, 20
101st New York, 72
104th Ohio Volunteers, 20
108th New York, 60
111th Pennsylvania, 60
141st New York, 51, 53
142nd New York, 21
154th New York, 51
155th Pennsylvania, 154
195th Pennsylvania Regiment, 143
Opera, description of, 73–74

Pallas, 66
Pamlico Sound, 10, 118
Pardons, 144–145
Parker, Charley, 11
Patent Office, xvi, 71, 122
    hospital at, 17, 27–28
Pennsylvania
    Cumberland Valley, 39
    Philadelphia, 143
    Reedsburg, 154
    Shenandoah Valley, 143
    Tidioute, 60
Petersburgh, Battle of, 137, 142
Physical health, correlation with spiritual
    well-being, xvii–xviii
Poplar Grove, Battle of, 106
Port Hudson, 93
Potomac, Army of the, xvi, 12, 88
Potter, Lt. Col., 10, 12
Prentiss, Col. Clifton, 137
Prisoners, 108–109

Ragan, James, 154
Rapidan River, 84
Rappahannock River, 11–12
Redgate, Stephen, 46
Rhodes, John, 38
Roberts, Milton, 63

Russell, Fred and Charley, 57

Sacrifice, xvii
2nd District Colored Regiment, 153
2nd Maryland, 137
2nd New Jersey Volunteers, 18
2nd New York Artillery, 145
2nd New York Cavalry, 68, 70
2nd Pennsylvania Cavalry, 39
2nd Pennsylvania Volunteers, 104
2nd Tennessee Volunteers, 61
2nd U.S. Artillery, 42
2nd U.S. Cavalry, 60
2nd U.S. Infantry, 154
2nd Virginia Regiment, 136
Sedgwick, Gen. John, 82, 84
Seven Days Fight, 142
17th Connecticut, 25
17th Pennsylvania Cavalry, 47
78th New York, 46
Seward, Secretary of State William, 25,
    32–33
Sheridan, Gen. Philip, 135
Sherman, Gen. William, 132, 136
Sims, Capt. S., 10, 12
6th Maryland Infantry, 137
Slave states, will of, 3
Small, Marcus, 18
Smith, Bethuel, 60
Smithsonian Institution, 34
Soldiers, 36. *See also* Black soldiers;
    Wounded soldiers
    in review, 135–136
Soldier's Home, 47, 56
"Song of Myself," xiv
South Carolina
    Charlestown Harbor, 3
    Columbia, 107
Spaulding, Jarvis, 21
Spiritualism, 89–90
Spiritual well-being, correlation with
    physical health, xvii–xviii
Stansbury, Michael, 118
Stanton, Secretary of War Edwin, 32, 57,
    136
Stanton Hospital, 145

Index

Strong, Lorenzo, 58
Suffering, xv–xvi, 76
Sullivan, Thomas, 38
Sumner, Gen. Charles, 13, 25–26, 33
Susquehanna River, 48
Swiers, Joseph, 154

Tennessee, Columbia, 79
3rd Virginia Cavalry, 137
Thomas, Gen. George, 136
27th Indiana, 60

United States. *See* America

Venus, 129
Vicksburgh, Battle of, 93, 142
Virgil, 31
Virginia, 82–83
    City Point, 108
    Culpepper, 68, 82–86
    Eastville, 153
    Falmouth, 8–9, 17, 23, 32, 68
    Fredericksburg, 8–9
    Richmond, 21, 61, 95, 99–100, 142, 146
    Roanoke, 10
    Upperville, 79, 149
    Warrenton, 68
Virtue, of ordinary people, xvii

Wales, Prince of, 128
Walker, Filibuster, 128
Wallace, Jonathan and Susan, 146
Walt Whitman and the Civil War, xix
Walt Whitman's Civil War, xix
War Department, 20
Wartime letters, xviii
Washington, D.C., 75, 114
    character of, 32–34, 43, 63, 120, 123–124,
        148–149
    Eighth Street, 17
    Fourteenth Street, 4–5, 48–49, 67, 114
    H Street, 17
    K Street, 57, 122
    Lafayette Square, 57
    military hospitals in, xv–xvi, 27
    Pearl Street, 7

(*Washington, D.C., cont'd.*)
    Pennsylvania Avenue, 4–5, 34, 37, 49,
        69, 71, 90, 96, 135, 138
    Seventh Street, 67, 71, 135
    Sixth Street, 69
    troops pouring into, 4–6
Washington Monument, 34
Webster, Daniel, 128
White House, 26, 120, 124
White Oaks Church, Battle of, 63–64
Whitman, Capt. George Washington,
    xiv–xv, xviii, 8, 92, 96, 105–108, 113, 120,
    126, 142
Whitman, Walt
    faith in democracy, xiv–xv
    health of, xvi, 51, 66–67, 101–102, 118
    letters by, xviii, 51–54, 70, 133–134,
        139–140
    love of music, 55–56, 73–74
    newspaper career, xiv, xvii
    patriotism of, xiii, 91, 132, 142–143,
        154–155
    perspective on Civil War, xiv
    philosophy of, xiii–xiv, 37, 39, 134
    plans to lecture, 44
    poetry of, xiii, xvii, 75, 88, 113
    prose writings of, xviii–xix
    self-descriptions, 33–35, 41, 70, 103
    stories told to, 7, 12
    upbringing, xiv
    on visiting hospitals, xv–xvi, 30, 39–41,
        52–53, 55, 61, 154
Wilber, Oscar F., 51
Wilderness Campaign, 142
Williams, James, 137
Winder, Joseph, 153
Wound-Dresser, The, xix
Wounded soldiers, 31–32
    demeanor of, xii–xiii
    reaching out to, 22, 76, 119
    visitors to, 27
Wright, Maj. John, 107
Wyckoff, Nicholas, 38

About the Editor

JOHN HARMON McELROY is professor emeritus of American literature at the University of Arizona. He has also held faculty appointments at Clemson University and the University of Wisconsin and has been a Fulbright professor of American studies at universities in Brazil and Spain. His other books are the authoritative edition of Washington Irving's *Life and Voyages of Christopher Columbus, Finding Freedom: America's Distinctive Cultural Formation,* and, most recently, *American Beliefs: What Keeps a Big Country and a Diverse People United.*

The Sacrificial Years

was set in Adobe Caslon. Designed and cut by William Caslon in the 1720s and 1730s, the original Caslon types are some of the best-loved text faces. They have been copied and reinterpreted for over two centuries, their unrivaled success due to the exceptional readability of the type. While a close look at individual letters reveals eccentricities, a distinctive and friendly charm emerges when they are woven into a texture of words on a printed page. The present version, designed directly in the digital medium and modeled on the letters cut by Caslon in the early 18th century (rather than on later interpretations for letterpress or photo-typsetting), was created for Adobe Sytems by Carol Twombly.

Book design by Mark Polizzotti